Muslims, Schooling and the Question of
Self-Segregation

Muslims, Schooling and the Question of Self-Segregation

Shamim Miah
Senior Lecturer, University of Huddersfield

First published 2015 by
PALGRAVE MACMILLAN

Palgrave Macmillan in the UK is an imprint of Macmillan Publishers Limited, registered in England, company number 785998, of Houndmills, Basingstoke, Hampshire RG21 6XS.

Palgrave Macmillan in the US is a division of St Martin's Press LLC, 175 Fifth Avenue, New York, NY 10010.

Palgrave Macmillan is the global academic imprint of the above companies and has companies and representatives throughout the world.

Palgrave® and Macmillan® are registered trademarks in the United States, the United Kingdom, Europe and other countries.

ISBN 978–1–137–34775–6

This book is printed on paper suitable for recycling and made from fully managed and sustained forest sources. Logging, pulping and manufacturing processes are expected to conform to the environmental regulations of the country of origin.

A catalogue record for this book is available from the British Library.

A catalog record for this book is available from the Library of Congress.

In memory of my late father, Sujat Miah

Negro children needed neither segregated schools nor mixed schools. What they need is education.

W.E.B. Du Bois, 1868–1963

Contents

Tables

Acknowledgements

This book would not have been possible without the help, support and guidance from family (my mother and sisters), teachers and friends. Over the last two decades I have been fortunate enough to benefit from advice and direction from a number of people: in particular, Maxine Donnelley and other members of staff at the Black Access course at Manchester College (MANCAT) during the early 1990s for their guidance and inspiration – I thank you for teaching us that the impossible is possible. Atif Imtiaz (Cambridge) for his time and counsel; Sheikh Muhammad Mansur (Cardiff) for his help in thinking through the finer points of Muslim jurisprudence associated with Muslims in the West; Ziauddin Sardar for his encouragement; and Virinder Kalra (Manchester) for acting as a friend – for which I am eternally grateful. Special thanks to Mark Halstead, Emma Salter and Paul Thomas for sharing their wealth of knowledge and experience and their guidance.

I would also like to thank the following people who have helped, encouraged and supported me through the years. Afruz Ali, Jahangir Akhtar, Sadek Hamid and Shofique Ullah were there before it all began. Bodrul Alam, Akal Miah, Motlib Miah and others were significant during my formative years at 120 Chadderton Way. Special appreciation is also extended to Father Phil Sumner, Rev. Howard Sutcliffe, Steve Longdon, Salik Rahman, Barinur Rashid, Lebu Miah, Fazal Rahim and Mufti Helal Mahmood. My deepest appreciation is reserved for Nanu Miah for his support and encouragement – I hope our friendship strengthens with time.

Most significantly, my greatest debt is to my wife, Shefa, and children, Talha, Hannah and Musa. Without their patience and sacrifice, this book would not have seen the light of day.

Introduction

> Intellectuals are of their time, heralded along by the mass politics of representations ... capable of resisting those only by disputing the images, official narratives, justifications of power circulated by an increasingly powerful media – and not only media, but trends of thought that maintain the status quo, keeping things within acceptable and sanctioned perspective on actuality by ... unmasking or alternative versions in which to the best of one's ability the intellectual tries to tell the truth ... This is not always a matter of being a critic of government policy, but rather thinking of the intellectual vocation as maintaining a state of constant alertness, of a perpetual willingness not to let half-truths or received ideas steer one along.
>
> (Edward Said 1994:16–17)

Since the start of the first decade of the twenty-first century the concerns over Muslims communities, schooling and integration have never been far from Britain's political and media debates. The racial disturbances in some northern mill towns and cities such as Oldham, Burnley and Bradford in the summer of 2001 saw young Muslim men of Asian heritage routinely clash with police and white young men from neighbouring wards. Images of these clashes prompted significant concerns amongst politicians and the media. The government took the view that the riots were caused by the existence of spatial 'self-segregation' whereby distrust of wider communities was set off by the lack of social contact between the various communities. The

1

events of 9/11 and the subsequent bombings in London in July 2005 (7/7) by four young men, most of them born and educated in the UK, helped to consolidate a 'worrying' level of concern regarding the nature of Muslim communities in general and young Muslims in particular around the nexus of hyper-masculinity, anti-liberalism and violent extremism. The government responded to these 'concerns' by re-focusing state policy away from multiculturalism and community cohesion and towards a counter-terrorism agenda based upon a logic which argued that if *spatial* self-segregation led to the 2001 civil disturbances then *cultural* self-segregation led to violent extremism which culminated in the London bombings.

Since the mass migration of Muslims to Britain following the Second World War, a number of policy measures have been introduced by the government to govern Muslim communities. They began initially as short-lived policies addressing assimilation during the 1950s and early 1960s. This was followed by a Jenkinsian approach to integration based upon 'cultural diversity in an atmosphere of mutual tolerance' (Jenkins 1967); this opened up the discussions on multiculturalism that emphasised public recognition of cultural difference through government policy. Following the critical events of the 2001 riots and 7/7 London bombings there has been a significant shift away from multiculturalism towards policies on integration based upon community cohesion (Cantle 2005) and tackling of radical extremism (Thomas 2011). It was argued that not only did policies of multiculturalism facilitate an idea of separateness – the cultural and spatial separatism which have helped alienate generations of Muslims from British society – but this has also acted as a conduit for Islamic radicalism (Nazir-Ali 2008). This has signalled a call for Muslims to integrate into British mainstream society. One of the key areas in which this call has been articulated is education and schooling, while the shift to an emphasis on 'British values' has been signified by a debate on the 'death of multiculturalism'. The schooling of Muslim pupils and the educational choices of Muslim parents are seen as one of the principal ways through which this segregation is maintained and sustained. Some of the many concerns over 'segregation' of Muslim communities were predicated upon the fears around racial tensions (Cantle 2005), radicalisation of Muslim communities (Taylor 2009) and rejection of secular liberalism (MacEoin 2005). These policy debates within the last decade have played a significant role in the way in which Muslims are positioned. It is often argued that not only have Muslims failed to integrate into mainstream British society, but rather they have taken active steps to segregate themselves. They have, moreover, chosen to use state schools not only to promote a narrow form of cultural conservatism but also to embed social and cultural isolation with ephemeral connections to the wider host society.

Despite the endless public debate and government concerns over both Muslim faith schools, as seen in the Derby Muslim school controversy, and state schools, as witnessed in the Trojan Horse saga (see Chapter 1), little empirical research has been conducted to examine the question of self-segregation or, more crucially, how these national policy debates are understood, discussed and debated by Muslim communities. This book aims to address this lacuna by drawing upon empirical research with Muslim parents and pupils in state compulsory education and also the Muslim independent school sector in order to assess and evaluate the meaning and practice of integration within the context of schooling. In doing this it will attempt to critique the following commonly held popular assumptions and beliefs on Muslim self-segregation and schooling: to what extent do Muslim parents use education as an inoculating process against Western liberalism? Do Muslim parents self-consciously choose to educate their children within a Muslim environment? Are pupils attending Muslim schools less prepared for citizenship in secular Western societies? Are integrated or ethnically mixed schools the best policy option for tackling 'ethnic sectarianism'? Do ethnically segregated schools undermine religious tolerance and can they promote violent extremism? More crucially, is there a disconnect between educational policy discourses on integration and schooling and the lived experiences of Muslims?

A book which is grounded upon empirical study of Muslims and schooling is particularly timely, especially given the media attention and discursive policy positioning of Muslims in Britain. There is also a paucity of literature on how Muslim communities conceptualise and visualise the ongoing debate on segregation, integration and schooling. The robust educational policy imperative which has emerged during the last decade has attempted to address the 'Muslim problematic' through ethnic integration, segregation and de-radicalisation policies.

The absence of empirical work on Muslim discourses on integration and schooling, especially during this racially tense period with attempts at 'preventing violent extremism' through government policy, is a major concern for all of us. Academics, researchers and students will, it is hoped, find this book useful, as it assesses the impacts of policies on integration and schooling for Muslims and also wider society within a heightened security context. For policy analysts, educationalists or people working with Muslim communities, this book will offer a detailed and complex interpretation of integration/segregation and schooling by parents and pupils alike. It attempts to show how the Muslim discourse of integration and schools moves beyond the typical binary approach to integration and segregation. Instead it argues for a shift away from a Manichean framing of integration and segregation within the context of schooling by drawing upon empirical data which support the claim that, for Muslim pupils and parents, neither integration nor segregation is important. What matters is education.

The question of reflexivity is paramount to any academic research. The potential impacts of the researcher's own worldview on data collection and interpretation are an important strand in any given research. Positionality, or the location of the self, is central to assessing the question of validity. Thus it is not surprising to see that a number of scholars have stressed the importance of considering one's 'own positionality' (Jackson 1993, cited in Hopkins 2007) and the 'politics of positions' (Rose 2007, cited in Hopkins 2007) during the research process. In short, there can be 'seen, unseen and unforeseen' hazards when researchers 'do not pay attention to their own and others' racialized and cultural systems of coming to know…the world' (Millner 2007:387). In researching this project, the issue of positionality and reflexivity has been a central component. I am conscious of the fact that I am a Muslim of Bangladeshi origin, born in the UK. I have been a school governor for ten years and have also served as a member of Oldham's Standing Advisory Council for Religious Education (SACRE) for over ten years. Currently I am serving as chair of governors in an ethnically mixed secondary school. I have also over ten years' experience of grassroots working in my voluntary capacity as a community activist, including serving as the Chair of the Oldham Inter-faith Forum. Researching the Muslim communities in light of this experience brought about certain advantages through 'alliance formation' (Harvey 1996:360) and developing rapport and shared experiences (Hopkins 2007). My research positionality also carried certain privileges. Prior to taking up an academic post, I had worked for eight years as a local government policy analyst in the field of equality and social policy. It was my voluntary experience that initially motivated me to research the question of Muslims, schooling and self-segregation. Having spent long hours attending community meetings, speaking to parents, community activists and faith leaders, I was able to detect a disconnect between political and policy rhetoric and the everyday lived realities of Muslim communities. When I embarked on my academic career my challenge was to conduct a detailed empirical academic research to analyse and assess some of the underlying issues by broadening the field of research to include other towns and cities including London, Blackburn, Burnley, Leeds and Manchester. I also sought to widen the sample groups to include Muslims from the Indian subcontinent, Muslims of Arab and African descent and convert Muslim communities.

My interest in the works of the late Edward Said helped provide some theoretical context. Said was one of the early intellectuals to provide a detailed critique of the representation of the essentialised representation of the 'other' in a number of western canonical texts. In the quotation taken from *Representation of the Intellectual*, based upon his BBC Reith lectures in 1993, Said notes how it is the role of the intellectual to assess events not from the viewpoint of the ivory tower, but rather through endeavouring to provide alternative views to received wisdoms, challenging the official narratives and trends which help maintain a particular status quo. For Said (1993) there is no question that 'the intellectual belongs on the side of the weak and unrepresented' (Said 1993:17) and that the 'intellectual representations are the activity itself, dependent upon the kind of consciousness that is sceptical, engaged, unremittingly devoted to rational investigation and moral judgment' (Said 1993:15).

Chapter summaries

Chapter 1 aims to provide a broad context to the current debate on Muslims, schooling and segregation by exploring how the idea of spatial and cultural self-segregation evolved in public and policy discourses. It will show that while the antecedents of the concept can be traced back prior to the Rushdie Affair, the contemporary framing of segregation (particularly spatial segregation) takes a consolidated form following the 2001 race riots. Following the 7/7 London bombing and subsequent debates on extremism and violent extremism, cultural segregation becomes the dominant motif for framing the Muslim problematic.

Chapter 2 examines the diverse ways the concept is debated within political discourses. It shows how political actors ranging from Tony Blair and Gordon Brown to David Cameron have responded to the question of segregation through the ideas of Britishness, which maintain that minority ethnic cultures should respect and accept key fundamental and non-negotiable values as a demonstration of loyalty and citizenship. This chapter will also offer a critique of this rhetorical framing of Britishness by demonstrating how contemporary political discourses are underpinned by a neoliberal assimilationist paradigm, which marks a fundamental shift away from cultural pluralism towards an assimilationist agenda. The chapter concludes by demonstrating how there is very little consensus over the term 'integration', showing instead how the concept is ambiguous, vague, obscure and, above all, open to criticism. More crucially, it argues that political discourse has led to the demonisation and pathologisation of Muslims, which has further marginalised Muslim communities.

Chapter 3 examines the policy debate on segregation and schooling with particular emphasis on *spatial narratives* associated with neighbourhoods with high concentrations of Muslim communities. It takes the 2001 race riots as a pivotal milestone event for the introduction of the community cohesion agenda. It further examines how the 7/7 bombings ushered in the agenda addressing the prevention of violent extremism within the wider education and schooling debate. This chapter argues that a more active and aggressive policy was adopted under New Labour and continued by the Tory-led coalition government in 2010 to bring about 'forced integration' (Miah 2012) by merging state schools with significant proportions of Muslim pupils with white pupils. This chapter challenges some of the political underpinnings of such approaches to integration by arguing how they reflect an 'aggressive majoritarianism' (Gilborn 2008) approach rather than a desire to create a 'common school' (Levinson 2008; Pring 2008) based on liberal principles of equality, social justice and fairness. It further maintains how such approaches to integration will undermine social contact between ethnic groups.

Part II moves away from political and policy discussions towards empirical research conducted with Muslim pupils and parents in a number of cities with large Muslim communities, including Oldham, Burnley, Blackburn, Leeds, Manchester and London. Some of these towns and cities, underpinned by particular spatial narratives, hit the national headlines due to the 2001 riots, namely Oldham and Burnley. Leeds attracted international media attention due to the fact that most of the 7/7 bombers were educated and worked there. Blackburn also launched a national debate on religion, clothing and cultural self-segregation following the former Secretary of State Jack Straw's comments on the wearing of the veil in public spaces. Part II offers new ways of conceptualising the debate on integration. As a result, it brings to the foreground some of the national and local debates on integration, Muslim communities and schooling.

Chapter 4 challenges the idea of self-segregation by exploring how Muslim pupils in ethnically mixed schools frame the question of integration and segregation. Chapter 5 deconstructs the idea of Muslim spatial-segregation by demonstrating how Muslim communities are far from static, unchanging monoliths; but rather best described as shifting geographies of ethnic settlement, symbolised by the movement (or desire to move) out of traditional areas into ethnically mixed and diverse neighbourhoods. Chapter 6 challenges the idea of cultural segregation by drawing upon focus group and one-on-one interviews with Muslim pupils who have attended (or are currently attending) Muslim faith schools by providing a counter-narrative to the popular logic that 'Muslim schools leads to segregation', or that Muslim parents' intention of sending pupils to these schools is based on the desire of nurturing cultural separatism. Instead, it will argue that the best way to understand faith schools is through a paradoxical lens, whereby the parental desire for Muslim faith school education is based upon the idea of integration through faith. Chapter 7 demonstrate how ethnically segregated or integrated schools are determined by parental social class positionality. Chapter 5 shows how *some* Muslim parents, empowered through their economic capital, not only desire but actively pursue the course of integration; this recognition and affirmation of integration is an important mechanism through which status is gained within the community. Conversely,

Chapter 7 argues how *class segregation* grounded upon the ideas of inequality, poverty and lack of opportunity means that parents who want to send their children to high-achieving ethnically mixed schools are unable to do so.

Drawing upon primary source data, this book aims to uncover a Muslim perspective on segregation by providing a space for Muslims to articulate what integration and the politicised debate of segregation/integration means to them. As already stated, the Muslim voice is an important research topic, not only to guide the principles of equality and democracy, but also to inform academic debates on how normative constructs of religion, migration and race relations are contested and challenged. For the purpose of this study the concept of self-segregation will be understood as a discursive category; emphasis will be placed on what ethnic segregation within the context of schools means to the Muslim community. It is envisaged that an understanding of what integration means to the Muslim community will not only help inform public policy discourses on integration, but also provide an understanding of the sociology of education of Muslim pupils in Britain. In summary, this book argues against the premise that Muslims in Britain want to live in self-segregated communities determined by spatial and cultural self-segregation. Furthermore, it refutes the claim implicit in both policy and political discourses that Muslim communities actively develop conscious racial boundaries with a willingness to create their own physical and cultural ghettos as a way of maintaining an essentialised 'Muslimness'.

Part I

1
Self-Segregation and the Muslim Problematic

> There has been a worldwide resurgence of the ideology of Islamic extremism. One of the results of this has been to further alienate the young from the nation in which they were growing up and also to turn already separate communities into 'no-go' areas where adherence to this ideology has become a mark of acceptability... Those of a different faith or race may find it difficult to live or work there because of hostility to them and even the risk of violence... Attempts have been made to impose an 'Islamic' character on certain areas.
>
> (Bishop Michael Nazir-Ali 2008)

The debate on Muslims and the question of self-segregation has become a dominant discourse shaping Muslim geographical space in the UK (Cantle 2005; Thomas 2011), and also in a range of other European countries such as France (Bowen 2007; Laborde 2008). A number of high-profile media stories have contributed towards a moral panic, with Muslim communities as the new folk devil (Cohen 2011). In fact these moral panics can be grouped together as *spatial* and *cultural* self-segregation. Spatial segregation revolves around a number of themes associated with ethnic residential clustering and 'Muslim no-go areas', which are symbolised by purpose-built mosques. It focuses on the idea that Muslims self-consciously live in separate neighbourhoods by deliberately excluding themselves from the rest of the society, by either actively resisting non-Muslims from entering their space or 'regulating' non-Muslim activities within 'Muslim areas'. The creation of 'Muslim ghettoes' has been fuelled

11

by recent sensationalist headlines over the 'Shari'a patrols' of inner-city Muslim neighbourhoods. The Shari'a patrols refer to videos uploaded to YouTube by self-proclaimed Muslim vigilantes patrolling the streets of East London, confronting non-Muslims consuming alcoholic drinks and ordering women to dress appropriately by proclaiming that 'this is a Muslim area' (Gadher 2013). Whilst these incidents were carried out by only a handful of Muslim men and were condemned by leading Muslims, including the East London Mosque (East London Mosque 2013), nevertheless the image of 'Muslim separatism' was reinforced in the public imagination, despite similar 'Christian patrols' conducted by the British far-Right group Britain First (Elgot 2014). Whilst spatial segregation revolved around the notion that Muslims want to construct *physical* barriers between Muslims and the rest of the population, cultural segregation refers to *mental* barriers shaped by certain cultural practices. A number of media stories and national debates have fuelled a debate on cultural self-segregation associated with the practice of endogamy (Kelly 2011; Peach 2006), wearing of the Niqab in public spaces (Straw 2006), growing concerns over sharia courts in Britain (Bano 2012; Corbin 2013) and the practice of *biraderi* politics influencing democratic practices (Akhtar 2003).

This particular discourse has evolved over the years in regard to its initial concern with spatial and residential segregation changing to more perceived cultural forms of segregation which reached particular prominence following the events of the London bombings. In response to the shifting paradigms, the policy measures aimed at responding to these 'problems' also shifted away from community cohesion to prevention of violent extremism.

This chapter aims to provide a broader context to the question of Muslim self-segregation within educational debate; it aims to provide the reader with an idea of how particular events have shaped our understanding of Muslim communities in Britain. It also contextualises not only how the question of self-segregation is problematised, but also how this problematisation has evolved and consolidated within political and policy discourse.

Cultural separatism as 'purdah mentality'

For some observers the question of Muslim self-segregation is a problem that has recently gained prominence after the London bombings in 2005 and took a consolidated form after the Trojan Horse story connected with Birmingham state schools. In reality the debate on integration, Muslims and schooling in Britain has a long and complex history, which can be traced back to the early 1980s with the Ray Honeyford affair in Bradford, the Alvi sisters' hijab controversy in Altrincham, Cheshire, during the late 1980s and, more crucially, the debates connected with state funding of Muslim state schools during the late 1980s and early 1990s.

Ray Honeyford (1983a; 1983b; 1984) became a *cause célèbre* for the New Right after publishing a number of articles questioning multicultural educational orthodoxies of Bradford City Council, in a series of articles published in the *Times Education Supplement* (Honeyford 1983b) and most significantly for the *Salisbury Review* (Honeyford 1984) – a political journal associated with the New Right. Honeyford, head teacher of the Drummond Middle School in Bradford with a majority Muslim cohort, viewed Muslims through an essentialised lens of *cultural separatism*, which he felt was akin to 'imposing purdah mentality in schools'. For Honeyford, Muslim community, culture and religion were diametrically opposite to the reified British culture and his fundamental principle revolved around the ways in which the antiquated nature of Pakistani Muslim culture were unable to cope with 'democracy' and the 'rule of law'. More crucially he felt that principles of multiculturalism which allowed a 'growing number of Asians whose aim is to preserve as intact as possible the values and attitudes of the Indian subcontinent within a framework of British social and political privilege, i.e. to produce Asian ghettos' (Honeyford 1984). Whilst the New Right championed Honeyford for his attack on multicultural education policy and obscurantist Muslim culture, the political Left described him as a racist bigot and a mouthpiece for the political Right. After a coordinated campaign Honeyford was suspended as the head teacher, but following an appeal to the High Court he was reinstated (Halstead 1988). However, in light of mobilised pressure by parent groups and national anti-racist organisations, Honeyford was forced to take early retirement. Some 25 years after the Honeyford controversy, he was seen to be vindicated by the national media and senior politicians. Whilst during the 1980s multiculturalism exerted a degree of influence in framing education policy and Muslim communities, following riots in 2001 not only was the multicultural consensus questioned but also the 'death of multiculturalism' was advocated. The re-imaging of Honeyford as 'the man who predicted the Race Riots' and a person 'if we had only listened to…we should have not sown what we are now reaping and what we (and others) shall reap for many years to come' (Darlymple 2002) shows the journey that British race relations discourses has made from the political Left to a secure position on the centre Right.

The public debate surrounding cultural segregation was to hit the national and international headlines once again during the late 1980s after Altrincham Grammar School for Girls, one of the best grammar schools in Britain, suspended two Muslim sisters for wearing the hijab on the grounds of cultural integration (Alvi 2010). This event brought the questions of secularism, conspicuous religious symbolism and religious tolerance into the national debate in Britain some 25 years before the Stasi Commission report in France, which ultimately led to the banning of the hijab in French schools. Unlike the French judgement, the Altringham Grammar School affair, following a national campaign supported by diverse groups including the Commission for Racial Equality, Manchester Council of Mosques, the *Jewish Gazette* and the National Union of Teachers, led to an out-of-court settlement with the family of the Alvi sisters, in light of changes to the school's uniform policy. More recently, the case of Shabina Begum and Denbigh High School in Luton has demonstrated the evolving conflicts regarding Muslim dress code, school policy and the nature of secular space (Ward 2006; Idris 2006; Singh and Cowden 2011). The Shabina Begum controversy began during the new school year in 2002. Like most secondary schools in Britain, Denbigh High School had in place a school policy that accommodated Muslim girls by allowing them to wear the traditional shalwar kameez, comprising loose trousers and tunic, together with the hijab. Shabina Begum argued that this policy did not meet her strict religious needs because the shalwar kameez reflected the cultural legacy of the Indian subcontinent, including that of Hindu and Sikh girls. Instead, Ms Begum chose to wear the jilbab – a long, loose garment worn by Muslim women throughout the Middle East and which she considered met the criteria of Islamic dress. Ms Begum refused to attend the school and, with the help of her family, issued a judicial review seeking a declaration that the school had unlawfully denied her the right to manifest her religion and, as a result, had denied her right to education (Idris 2007). The High Court rejected the judicial review in June 2004 on the grounds that neither had her religious freedoms been breached nor had she been excluded from the school (Ward 2006). In light of this judgement Ms Begum took the matter to the Court if Appeal, which in March 2005 offered a different response to that of the High Court, arguing instead that Denbigh High School 'approached the issues...from an entirely wrong direction and did not attribute claimant's beliefs the weight they deserved' (cited in Idris 2007). Ms Begum's fate was finally determined by an appeal made by the school at the House of Lords, which ruled in favour of Denbigh High School and provided a similar judgement to that of the High Court by arguing that Ms Begum's religious freedoms had not been violated and that Denbigh High School – with a signifi- cant number of Muslim students (79 per cent), including a Muslim head teacher – had a comprehensive uniform policy (Idris 2007). Ms Begum's case is significant not because it signifies conflict between Muslims and secular space; rather it demonstrates an internal debate and difference over the requirements and authenticity of religious dress.

The subject of cultural self-segregation was a dominant feature in the discussions over state funding of Muslim faith schools from the mid-1980s onwards; the provisions for religious faiths to establish schools which are recognised and funded by the state have been utilised by both Christian and Jewish communities since the intro- duction of the 1944 Education Act. The emphasis on single-gender education, the importance of preserving ones cultural and religious identity and providing a safe space were the initial drivers behind the establishment of Muslim faith schools. This meant that Muslim schools were increasingly viewed through the lens of 'separatism'. The fact that Muslims were requesting an extension of existing pro- visions enjoyed by other religious groups was disregarded; instead the confident display and expression of Muslim identity within the public space was seen as a particular threat to the Judeo-Christian consensus. The emergence of an active voice for state funding of Muslim schools coincided with the growth of national educational groups, academic organisations and Muslim representative bodies, including the Muslim Educational Trust (1966), The Islamic Academy (1983), the *Muslim Education Quarterly* (1983) and the Association of Muslim Schools (1992). At the local level, as early as January 1983, the Muslim Parents Association in Bradford submitted a proposal to

Bradford Local Education Authority that, given the absence of single-sex schools and lack of religious provision for Muslim pupils, their association take control of five schools with the aim of running them staffed by voluntary aided schools (Haw 1994).

Assimilation or separation?

The significance of 'separate' educational provision within the national debate in Britain can be reflected by the rejection of the idea of 'separate' school provision by the Committee of Inquiry into the Education of Children from Ethnic Minority Groups, established by the government in 1979. The committee felt that 'separate provision' was fundamentally wrong for a diverse and multicultural society; rather, it argued that 'a degree of shared experience can be seen as one of the major factors in maintaining a cohesive society' (Swann 1985:5).

The question of cultural self-segregation during the 1980s was shaped by two crucial debates, the first being the history of the struggle against and resistance to racism within working-class 'Black' communities in Britain – the term 'Black' being understood as a political category rooted in the experiences of racism and imperialism by post-colonial subjects. This period witnessed active campaigning against street- and state-based racism together with the popular appeal of the Asian Youth Movements (Ramamathury 2013). Thus it is not surprising to note that some of the early demands for opting out of mainstream state provisions were grounded upon fears and concerns regarding racial harassment and institutional failures to embed anti-racist and anti-sexist educational policies (Haw 1994). The 1980s also witnessed the McDonald inquiry into racism and racial violence in Manchester schools linked to the murder of the Manchester schoolboy, Ahmed Iqbal Ullah, in a school playground in Burnage. This damning report provided systematic examples of racism by members of staff and pupils against Muslim youths, and also documented graphic examples of institutional forms of racism.

The second debate was in regard to the rejection of the policy of assimilation within public policy discourse which envisaged that the 'problem' of minority communities could be solved by full assimilation, whereby minority ethnic groups would be absorbed and subsumed within the host society (Swann Report 1985:1991). The Swann

Report (1985) considered neither of these options valid: the agenda of assimilation was seen as a 'denial of the fundamental freedom of all individuals to differ on aspects of their lives where no single way can justifiably be presented as universally appropriate' (Swann 1985:4). The report argued that such policies were 'unreasonable', 'unjust' and, above all, 'unrealistic'. Equally, a policy of separatism would 'offer equality or justice to the numbers of all groups, least of all the numerically smaller minorities' (Swann 1985:5).

Instead, the Swann Report (1985) proposed that a multicultural policy grounded on the idea of pluralism was a way out of this binary typology. It argued that, given the nature of a multi-racial society, a third way would be in the interests of that society as a whole and would, more importantly, be in tune with the changing nature of post-war Britain. It proposed that plural society:

> would function most...harmoniously on the basis of pluralism which enables...all members of all ethnic groups...to partici-pate in shaping the society as a whole within a framework of commonly accepted values, practices and procedures...In a demo-cratically pluralism society, we believe all members of that society, regardless of ethnic origin have an obligation to abide by the cur-rent laws of the country and to seek to change them only through peaceful means.
>
> (Ibid.)

Whilst the foregoing locates the self-segregation debate within a his-torical context, it also notes that the overcoming of 'problems' does not represent 'closure', but rather symbolises how future debates are framed. For example, a number of landmark victories for Muslims in regard to state education dating back to the 1980s, such as halal food provisions, school policies on Muslim dress and state fund-ing of Muslim schools, continue to dominate popular discourses on segregation and integration.

Sleepwalking into spatial self-segregation

The racial disturbances in some the northern English mill towns and cities such as Oldham, Burnley and Bradford in the summer of 2001 saw Muslim young men routinely clash with police and White young men from neighbouring wards. The images of violent clashes of young Muslim men of Asian heritage prompted significant concerns among politicians and the media. The riots were seen to be an outcome of an 'us and them' mentality caused in the main through the 'existence' of spatial self-segregation, whereby distrust of wider communities was due to lack social contact between the various communities. Whilst residential ethic segregation was one of the key features of the 2001 riots, the links between residential and educational segregation became a key feature in the public debate. These debates came on the back of a series of inquiries into the riots. Among the individuals and bodies to advocate this idea were Sir Herman Ouseley (2001), who discussed the 'virtual apartheid' nature of state schooling in Bradford; the Cantle Report (2001), which warned of 'parallel lives' created by the schooling system; and the Ritchie Report (2001), which encouraged Oldham to adopt policies that would lead to better integration and the desegregation of state schools. Indeed Ritchie (2001), drawing upon memories of both the Holocaust and Irish sectarianism between Catholics and Protestants, attempted to articulate the seriousness of ethnic self-segregation in the following:

In the course of preparing my parts of this report, I came across the following quotation by the Christian spiritual writer Donald Nicholl. Describing the relationship between different parts of society in Germany after the First World War he said 'The different religious and political groupings in Germany were so deeply divided that it would have been almost unthinkable – even impertinent – for a representative of one group to have spoken up on behalf of another group. To begin with, these groups virtually never met one another socially; Catholics went to Catholic schools and Protestants to Protestant schools; socialists had their comics for socialist children and communists had theirs for their children; Jews went to Jewish doctors and Catholics to Catholic doctors; all along the line they tended to meet only people of their own religious or political colour, whether they were worshipping or playing or being ill; and so they harboured the strangest notions about those outside their own community'. It would be an exaggeration to say that divisions in Oldham have reached the level described by Nicholl, but the lessons from that time remain ones which need always to be kept in mind. The fact that it is mainly *self-segregation* makes the task all the more challenging.

(Ritchie Report 2001:5–6, emphasis added)

The 2001 race riots marked a significant turning point in the policy debate on segregation and self-segregation. First, it represented not only a shift but also a firm rejection of multiculturalism as state policy. Second, it drew the conclusion, by echoing Honeyford's idea, that the state policy of multiculturalism was somehow responsible for civil unrest among communities. Finally, it challenged resources in state policies aimed at facilitating the 'death of multiculturalism'.

Multiculturalism, with cultural recognition through government policy and in regard to providing an equal say for minority groups, was seen as an inappropriate way of meeting the contemporary challenges arising from recent political events. It was argued that, hitherto, policies of multiculturalism had been promoting a sense of 'difference' which nurtured a sense of racial and religious 'separateness'. The concept of community cohesion was developed and promoted as a way of meeting the new challenges post-race riots and 9/11. The key task for multicultural societies was:

To come to terms with domains of difference and to develop a greater consensus ... bonds between fellow citizens require greater sense of commonality. Furthermore, agreement about how to achieve such a consensus will also be required and it is suggested that this will depend upon breaking down the separateness between the minority and majority community and between the different minority communities themselves. Mutual trust and common sense of belonging will only be created through constant interactions and shared experiences.

(Cantle 2008:12)

The community cohesion thesis, with its emphasis on shared values and social contact, was hugely influential in a number of towns and cities in the UK, especially in localities with a high concentration of black and minority ethnic communities in general and Muslim communities in particular. Community cohesion marked a different way in both conceptualising and responding to the question of self-segregation and parallel lives. In the context of schooling it nurtured the idea of cohesion both between and within schools. In dealing with the question of segregation between schools, a number of schools established the 'school linking' projects through the Schools Linking Network (SLN) (DoE 2010). The aim of the SLN is to pair different schools within the borough with different ethnic cohorts, aiming to 'facilitate links between schools…to help children and young people to explore their identity, celebrate diversity and develop dialogue' (DoE 2010:6). Whilst evaluation of the SLN in Bradford and London was broadly positive (ibid.), nevertheless the principles behind it are questionable and some of the issues are discussed in detail in Chapter 3. However, the broad ideas associated with community cohesion have been criticised for the following reasons: first, it assumes that some communities are more cohesive than others; it is often said that it is the Muslim communities that are more unwilling to integrate or mix with other communities. Second, for some critics the idea of community cohesion, conceptually speaking, 'represented an empty vessel into which the pre-occupations of contemporary public policy were poured' (Robinson 2005:1415). In other words, community cohesion is seen as a 'sound right' policy which provides a common-sense rather than empirical justification for policy intervention (ibid.). Third, community cohesion fails to respond to some of the challenging questions regarding how, within a multicultural, multi-ethnic and multi-faith society, one can achieve consensus over shared values (McGee 2003). Finally, the policies associated with community cohesion were short lived: following the unfolding of terrorist activities in the streets of London, the community cohesion mantra was quickly replaced by a more aggressive language of securitisation and counter-terrorism.

Multiculturalism as conduit for self-segregation

The 2001 race riots also witnessed a paradigm shift away from the politics of multiculturalism, which celebrated diversity and difference, towards policy framing around shared values and Britishness. British multiculturalism was no longer seen as ideal way of governing minority ethnic communities: rather, it was seen as being responsible for fostering social division, undermining national identity, nurturing domestic terrorism and, above all, creating self-segregation.

Whilst the 2001 race riots and the subsequent events surrounding domestic terrorism consolidated concerns and fears around multiculturalism and self-segregation, nevertheless some of these concerns predate these milestone events. The history of multiculturalism is long and complex; there are, however, some central features which revolve around the principle of cultural recognition. First, there is emphasis on the recognition at the level of state policy of cultural identity of minority and other underprivileged groups in society; and second, this failure to recognise cultural difference has socio-psychological implications for the individuals or groups concerned. Indeed, there is a long tradition within Western philosophy which recognises the importance of cultural difference with its emphasis on equal respect, human agency and self-expressive choice. For example, Taylor (1992) has long considered the importance of the 'politics of human dignity', which he argues is closely associated with equal worth and respect – equal worth and respect as a 'universal human potential' happens when each person is made to feel they deserve respect and recognition. One of the crucial elements of cultural difference is the need to recognise that human beings are born in and influenced by their cultural communities. Thus it is critical to appreciate the fact that cultural difference has value. For Taylor (1992:68), 'just as all must have equal civil rights and equal voting rights, regardless of race or culture, so all should enjoy the presumption that their traditional culture has value'. Not only do all cultures have value, they also start with the position of equal worth which demands recognition and nurture

The above approach to multiculturalism has had a significant impact on the way in which cultural difference is perceived and articulated by a range of academics and policy pundits. The conceptual framing of diversity as understood through the prisms of cultural recognition has policy implications for the way in which schools and the educational curriculum are constructed and administered based upon the objective of recognition of cultural difference in the ethos, curriculum and functioning of schools. One of the leading sociologists to engage with recent questions on multiculturalism and the Muslim problematic is Tariq Modood. Modood (2005) throughout his career has attempted to do this by articulating the recognition of Muslim communities within a secular liberal context. The question of Muslim integration should be understood within the context of multiculturalism or the 'politics of difference'. The politics of difference is not an individualised project but a collective group process.

Moreover, the politics of difference, for Muslims, means that it they align themselves to other minority groups, such as gender, race and sexuality – this, for Modood (2007), is the 3+1 principle. Muslim groups, according to this principle, are not requesting any additional rights but rather advocating that the same rights and recognition that have been granted to the three cited groups be extended to them. Thus:

> Marginalized and other religious groups, most notably Muslims, are now utilizing the same kind of argument and making the claim that religious identity, just like gay identity, and just like certain forms of racial identity, should not just be privatized or tolerated, but should be part of the public space.
>
> (Modood 2007:70)

The argument is rejected that Muslim identity cannot be associated with gender, sexuality or race because these are 'ascribed and involuntary' identities, whilst religious identity is essentially a matter of choice and therefore that religious groups should have less recognition, legal protection and claim on the public space. This argument is considered to be 'sociologically naive' because most Muslims have no choice in regard to being 'born into a Muslim family. Similarly, no one chooses to be born into a society where to look like a Muslim or to be a Muslim creates suspicion, hostility or failure to get a job you applied for' (Modood 2007:71). A key debate within the sociology of pluralism has challenged the conventional thinking of identity as implying sameness, stability and continuum with a central coherent essence which persists throughout one's life. Instead, research on identity has pointed out that it is a socially constructed phenomenon, which above all is fluid, adaptable and based upon notions of hybridity – thus identity is far from being 'fixed' but rather constantly in a state of flux (Hall 1992; Bhabha 1994). Thus identity is a construct and a process, which is never completed and is forever in the process of 'becoming'; it is a process steeped in the diasporic experience of minority communities and which has the ability to define and structure one's self in more than one way. This understanding is particularly relevant within the Muslim experience, especially in light of recent debates on European Muslim identity or Euro-Islam (Ramadan 1999, 2001, 2004, 2009a; March 2009a).

Following concerns over civil disorder, domestic terrorism and migration, the question of recognition of cultural diversity, group rights and dignity and respect was managed through the secular prism of liberalism. It was argued that the policy of multiculturalism not only nurtured self-segregation but, importantly, was detrimental to women. A number of issues have highlighted the assertive rejection of multiculturalism. In fact, recent concerns over multiculturalism have been predicated upon the idea of 'saving brown women from brown men'. The high-profile case of the murder of Shafilia Ahmed and her subsequent murder trial in 2012 raised the issue of 'honour killing' in general and forced marriage in particular. Shafilia Ahmed was a British Muslim girl of Pakistani heritage who was murdered by her parents, Iftikar and Farzana Ahmed, because of her rejection of an arranged marriage set up by her parents with a potential suitor in Pakistan. Shafilia's murder raised in the public imagination the conflicts between the demand of culture and tradition and the desire and the allure of Western lifestyle. Moreover, the practices of clitoridectomy, or female genital mutilation (FGM), in Britain have attracted much political attention. For example, despite FGM being illegal in Britain, according to a recent report 'more than 66,000 women in England and Wales have undergone FGM and more than 24,000 girls under the age of 15 are at risk of it' (Urquhart 2013). These cases have opened up much deeper questions relating to multicultural policy and its adverse impacts on women. In fact the critics of multiculturalism have long argued that most policies relating to multiculturalism protects the privileges and interests of men over women. It does this because most policies fail to recognise the private sphere of most minority cultural groups and the internal gender dynamics within such groups. More significantly, it is argued, such policies nurture self-segregation by exposing vulnerable groups within society through giving credence and legitimacy to cultural or traditional practices 'which aim to control women and render them, especially sexually and reproductively to men's desires and interest' (Okin 1999:16). A policy which pursues multiculturalism, it is argued, is not only 'bad for women', because most religious traditions in general and Islam in particular aim to control women and undermine their rights, but it also aims to undermine the spread of secular liberal democracies in the West.

The rejection of multiculturalism is not considered to undermine liberal values, but rather to strengthen enlightened values of rights for all and universal citizenship. This is because the premise of multiculturalism works on a 'rule and exception' model, where Muslims are given special rights (to slaughter animals) and given special exceptions (to wear a veil in public). It is argued that rules should be universal and be applied to all: this prevents specialist treatment and limits opportunities for conflict; furthermore, abandoning the idea of 'exceptions' will bring about better relations among religions (Barry 2001:50). As noted in the next chapter, David Cameron's (2011) ideas on 'muscular liberalism' are intended to secure the criminalisation of certain practices such as forced marriage and FGM, by stating that citizenship should be embedded upon certain non-negotiable secular liberal principles grounded on the famous maxim articulated by Karl Popper (d. 1994):

> We should therefore claim, in the name of tolerance, the right not to tolerate the intolerant. We should claim that any movement preaching intolerance places itself outside the law, and we should consider incitement to intolerance and persecution as criminal, in the same way as we should consider incitement to murder, or to kidnapping, or to the revival of the slave trade, as criminal.
> (Popper 1962 Vol. 1, Notes to the Chapters: Ch. 7, Note 4)

Self-segregation and violent extremism

Four British Muslims born, educated and brought up in Britain embarked upon a journey to London on July 2005 that would dramatically shift the way in which British Muslims are positioned within public discourse in general and government policies in particular. Three of the four – Hasib Hussain, Muhammad Siddique Khan and Shahzad Tanweer – were of Pakistani heritage while the fourth, Jermain Lindsay, of Jamaican heritage, was a convert to Islam; all four were considered to be Britain's 'home-grown terrorists' responsible for carrying out some of the worst acts of terrorism on mainland Britain.

One of the many questions arising from the London bombings was why seemingly 'normal' Muslim men born and educated in Britain would want to perpetrate such mass murder on its fellow citizens.

One of the answers to this question revolved around broader issues concerning loyalty, citizenship and patriotism. In fact the government applied the same logic of spatial segregation as noted in the 2001 race riots debate, leading to urban disorder, with the view that cultural self-segregation contributed towards the London bombings.

In response to the terrorism and extremism agenda, the government published one of its central programmes to tackle *violent* extremism. It recognised, in light of the taskforce report, that not all forms of extremism should be the target of policy – only violent forms. *Preventing Violent Extremism: Winning Hearts and Minds* was published by the Department of Communities and Local Government in April 2007. The Prevent approach was part of the CONTEST strategy, an overarching government approach to counter-terrorism initially developed in 2003 and later revised in 2006, 2009 and more recently in 2011.

As the title of the above Prevent programme demonstrates, the government was interested in turning the 'hearts and minds' of British Muslims away from the violent extremist narrative of Al-Qaeda. One of the central features of this government initiative is its discourse on integration which is articulated through the prism of shared values, Britishness and tackling segregation.

The Prevent strategy is seen by many as one of the key features of government counter-terrorism policies and it has come to reflect government's *soft* approach to counter-terrorism which aims at tackling self-segregation through education and community development. It is hoped that this approach will complement the government's *hard* approach, which involves responding to acts of criminal violence by the police, counter- terrorism officials and, most crucially, a raft of anti-terror legislations, including the Crime and Security Act 2001 (linked to internment of foreign national terror suspects), the Prevention of Terrorism Act 2005 (concerned with placing terror suspects under control orders) and the Terrorism Act 2006 (clamping down on extremist influences with the introduction of acceptable and unacceptable behaviours) (McGhee 2008).

The revised CONTEST strategy (HM Government 2009), otherwise known as CONTEST II, further intensified the grip on Muslim communities by extending surveillance and governance to target any verbal expression of dissent, in practice targeting any Muslim seen to be articulating illiberal views or questioning secular sentiments. This curtailment of any space for open debate was legitimated through an integrationist agenda, leading to a synthesis of counter-terrorism and tackling self-segregation:

> We will also continue to challenge views which fall short of supporting violence and are within the law, but which reject and undermine our shared values and jeopardise community cohesion – the strong and positive relationships between people of different ethnic, faith and cultural backgrounds in this country. Some of these views can create a climate in which people may be drawn into violent activity.
>
> (HM Government 2009:88)

The focus on Muslim communities shifted significantly from a legalistic approach to counter-terrorism as identified by CONTEST I (HM Government 2006), whereby the emphasis was placed upon tackling violent extremism, defined as actively promoting, propagating or participating in violent extremism. CONTEST II, however, viewed challenges to Britishness, secular liberalism or indeed shared values, which are perfectly legal, as equally reprehensible. Indeed the idea of shared values as a guiding principle of counter-terrorism strategy reflects wider political debate and a broader integration agenda within public discourse. Thus it wasn't surprising to note that the revised Prevent strategy published under the Tory-led coalition government in June 2011 further advocated the notion that the Al-Qaeda ideology can be challenged and undermined by the British ideology of shared values; moreover, it argued that 'Prevent depends upon a successful integration policy' (HM Government 2011:6). This they believe is based upon 'evidence' which demonstrates that 'support for terrorism is associated with rejection of a cohesive, integrated multi-faith society and parliamentary democracy' (HM Government 2011:5). It goes on to advocate that work 'to deal with radicalisation will depend on developing a sense of belonging to this country and support for our core values' (ibid.).

The Trojan Horse and 'Prevent'ing schooling

The merging of the Prevent agenda and school segregation took a consolidated form following the national debates on the Trojan Horse affair involving state schools with predominately Muslim areas in Birmingham.

In early March 2014 *The Sunday Times* covered a story which involved an 'Islamist plot to take over schools'; the story was based upon a leaked letter, which was initially sent to Birmingham City Council and was then sent to the Home Office after finally being leaked from the Department of Education. This letter, known as the Trojan Horse letter, referred to an alleged plot revolving around the idea of a 'radical Islamist plan' aimed at infiltrating schools with a majority of Muslim pupils, by transforming the leadership and management of these schools through recruiting 'hard-line Muslim parents and staff' with a view to implementing a narrow, ultra-conservative school curriculum (Miah 2014). This leaked correspondence, which was meant to have been written by 'Islamists' from Birmingham to fellow colleagues in Bradford and Manchester, encouraged Muslims to take over schools and to impose strict gender segregation within mixed co-educational secondary and primary schools.

As early as March 2014, serious flaws in the document started to emerge which questioned its authenticity, especially after it was revealed that the Trojan Horse letter may have been a hoax, connected to wider claims of fraud by former members of staff linked to one of schools mentioned in the letter – the links formed part of an investigation by the West Midlands Police (Oldham 2014). Despite the credibility of the letter or the claims made within it, the substance of the claim was internalised within public discourse, especially given that it appeared to conform to pre-existing ideas of Muslim communities, schooling and self-segregation.

In light of this, it is not surprising to note the reactions by the state. Both central and local government responses to the OTH – Operation Trojan Horse plot were to play a pivotal role in shaping the discursive parameters of the debate within counter-terrorism and securitisation. The city council responded by appointing Ian Kershaw as independent chief advisor with a view to overseeing the investigation. The Department of Education's response to dealing with the Trojan Horse story further consolidated the links between the Prevent agenda, self-segregation and schooling. The controversial response from Michael Gove, the Secretary of State for Education, was to appoint Peter Clarke, the former head of the Metropolitan

Police's counter-terrorism unit, which had led the investigations into the 7/7 London bombings in 2005. Gove also ordered the Office for Standards in Education (Ofsted) to conduct inspections on 21 state schools in Birmingham – all comprising wholly Muslim or majority Muslim cohorts, none of which were Muslim faith schools.

The Ofsted judgement, published in June 2014, further reinforced the links between segregation and state schooling. The approaches adopted by certain Ofsted examiners, together with the general consensus of all 21 inspection reports, led many to question the integrity, credibility and, above all, the independence of Ofsted. Of the 21 schools 6 were secondary, 1 all-through 4–19, 12 primary, 1 primary and nursery and 1 nursery. All these schools were publically funded and all were in deprived wards in Birmingham.

The main concern in all the Ofsted inspection reports revolved around the Prevent strategy (2011) rather than the comprehensive inspection framework identified in the *Ofsted Inspection Handbook*. In fact the *Ofsted Inspection Handbook* (revised April 2014) used by Ofsted inspectors makes no mention of the Prevent programme and the only cursory mention of 'preventing extremism' is part of wider discussion on 'the behaviour and safety of pupils at the school', which includes discussion on racism, e-safety and bullying.

In short, it seems that the inspection focused not on the quality of teaching and learning, nor on the bigger questions on equality of opportunity and outcome for inner-city poor children, but rather on the relationship between the Prevent agenda and the question of self-segregation. In fact one of the most striking cases involved Gracelands nursery school – the only nursery school on the list of 21 inspected by Ofsted. This nursery school had 52 pupils, all of whom were of South Asian heritage, and was criticised because 'school leaders were unaware of local authority or government guidelines on the prevention of extreme and radical behaviours as set out in the Prevent programme'. In light of this, Ofsted recommended that 'staff and governors require further and immediate training to ensure that the new policy is understood and appropriately monitored'. Part of this training, it was argued, would lead to 'identifying and minimising extremist behaviour' (Miah 2014). The embedding of the Prevent strategy raises a number of fundamental ethical questions. First, it seems that the indiscriminate use of Prevent measures was used to frame young Muslims, some as young as 4 years of age, through the lens of counter-terrorism. Second, one of the most significant moments in a child's memory of attending nursery starts with, as far as Ofsted is concerned, a deficit, or a label, which implies they are potential 'terrorists'. Third, from a practical point of view, how does Prevent operate within the context of early-years education? How are teachers to identify signs of radicalisation within nursery children? The significance of the Trojan Horse and Muslim participation in civic society in regard to the breakdown of trust can be seen by the resignation of the Board of Governors at Saltley School embroiled in the Trojan Horse scandal, due to 'little faith or trust' in the Ofsted inspection (Adams 2014).

The much-awaited publication of the Kershaw review (2014) on behalf of the city council and the Clarke report (2014) further helped reinforce the image of Muslim cultural separatism. The Clarke report (2014) highlighted 'intolerant and aggressive' Islamic ethos, and 'young people being encouraged to accept unquestionably a particular hard-line strand of Sunni Islam raises concerns about their vulnerability to radicalisation in the future' (Clarke 2014:13). The Kershaw review noted how some governors were determined to change the school to serve a particular Muslim worldview, often by breaking the law through not following the relevant protocols (Kershaw 2014:4). Despite these concerns, these reports have contradictory findings. For example, Kershaw (2014) maintains the view that some school governors used unacceptable practices as a way of raising standards, unlike Clarke (2014) who noted the presence of particularly hard-line aggressive governors. More crucially, Kershaw found 'no evidence of a conspiracy to promote an anti-British agenda, violent extremism or radicalisation in schools in East Birmingham' (Kershaw 2014:4).

Conclusion

The question of Muslim self-segregation and schooling has been of interest and a focus of public and policy debates going back to the early 1980s. The implicit assumption has been that since migration of Muslim communities since the 1960s has failed to integrate mainstream British society, they have chosen instead to live socially isolated and self-contained lives with ephemeral connections to the wider host society.

The first point to take from this chapter is that the problematisation of Muslims in Britain emerges through a series of events and conversations around the issues of spatial segregation, cultural segregation and self-segregation. Second, in light of socio-political and security, events at both international and domestic level have given way to policy approaches attempting to address the 'Muslim question' of self-segregation through a series of policies concerning counter-terrorism and desegregation. Third, debates on Muslim communities have a tendency to view the Muslim community as a monolith, an antiquated and obscurantist 'other' which not only attempts to preserve a sense of pristine Muslimness but also to impose this on its fellow believers. Finally, in recent years the question of self-segregation has taken a political form especially around the War on Terror and rise of global Muslim consciousness – this translates into pledging loyalty and sovereignty not to the nation state but rather to a collective body known as the 'Muslim Ummah'.

Despite many concerns and criticisms associated with the above positionality (Finney and Simpson 2009), popular discourses on segregation have further expressed the fear of 'Muslim ghettos' (Carey 2008) and 'no-go areas' (Nazir-Ali 2008) for White people in some northern towns, which it is argued can lead to reinforcing cultural difference and disloyalty towards the West. Segregated communities, parallel lives, Muslim ghettos and insular communities have subsequently become part of collective folk wisdom, which continues to influence political agendas in both the UK and other European Union (EU) countries with sizeable Muslim populations (Bowen 2007; Laborde 2008; Caldwell 2009).

These assumptions have also contributed towards the ways in which Muslim communities have been positioned. The educational policy imperative that has emerged during the last decade has attempted to address the 'Muslim question' within the education debate through both political discourses and a series of policy measures. Chapter 2 will explore the political discourses whilst Chapter 3 will examine the policy measures taken in response to the question of segregation.

2
Integration as Political Rhetoric

> This week there has been a big debate about British values
> following the Trojan Horse controversy in some Birmingham
> schools – about what these values are, and the role they
> should play in education. I'm clear about what these values
> are – and I'm equally clear that they should be promoted in
> every school and to every child in our country.
>
> (David Cameron 2014)

Chapter 1 highlighted how key events helped contextualise and
consolidate concerns regarding the question of Muslims, schooling
and self-segregation in both state schools and Muslim faith schools.
In light of these milestone events, this chapter focuses on the various
ways in which the state has reacted to these problems; it will demonstrate how both current and past prime ministers and senior political
actors have responded to these questions through the rhetorical discourse of Britishness, which is deeply influenced by assimilationist
repertoires. This discourse of Britishness maintains that minority
ethnic communities in general and Muslim communities in particular should respect and accept key fundamental and non-negotiable
values as a demonstration of loyalty and citizenship.

In the last decade there has been a consensus amongst both New
Labour and the coalition-led Tory government to frame the current
debate through the lens of Britishness by political actors as a way of
responding to and dealing with a range of problematic policy concerns. Social problems, such as segregation or violent extremism, are
seen as arising largely due to the weakening of collective identity
and poor sense of attachment to the neo-liberal state. These political

31

actors draw mainly on the communitarian approach (Etzioni 1993) which argues that a decline in moral standards and an increase in social ills are largely due to the expansion of citizens' rights. According to the communitarian logic, civil rights need to be balanced with responsibilities; it's only through a collective political project that the social problems in society can be addressed. This section examines the speeches made by leading UK politicians on tackling the question of segregation from the perspective of the value base of the host society. Whilst these approaches differ in both style and substance, it will be made clear that they envisage a singular narrative of Britain through a set of British values imposed upon migrant communities. Most of these approaches assert the idea that the Muslim question can be and should be addressed through an asserted emphasis on Britishness and shared values.

Blunkett and integration through citizenship

David Blunkett, the Home Secretary during the race riots of 2001, was one of the early pioneers of the use of shared values in addressing the question of integration. Blunkett's vision of integration can be found in the Crick Report (1998) which he commissioned. David Blunkett, a student of Bernard Crick, appointed the latter to head up an advisory group on citizenship education when Labour came to power in 1997. The Crick Report (1998) focused on the political notions of 'education for citizenship' for minority communities. This, he argued, is 'about learning laws, codes and conventions' or what Crick (1998) terms 'common citizenship'. Essentially, what the Crick Report was advocating was the importance of addressing the question of political apathy with regard to poor voter turnout during local and national elections. The report focused on pupils' understanding of political institutions in the UK and also on the importance of participating in political life through democracy and 'active citizenship', which Crick (1998) saw as volunteering, cooperation and participation in society.

The Crick Report (1998) was to have a significant influence on Blunkett; this is clear from the contents of the important White Paper and integration strategy published in 2002 – *Secure Borders, Safe Haven: Integration with Diversity in Modern Britain. Secure Borders, Safe Haven* sees the process of migration and globalisation as an inevitable reality of the modern world. In order to respond to these challenges, nation states need to ensure that integration of minority communities in general and an immigrant group in particular takes place. In order for this to happen, the Paper argues that 'we need to be secure within our sense of belonging and identity' and only through a collective shared identity will 'we' be able 'to embrace those who come to the UK' (Home Office 2002:1). The White Paper used the perspective of the Crick Report to place a strong emphasis on active citizenship based upon 'shared identity' and 'common values' (Home Office 2002:11). *Secure Border*s placed urgency upon active citizenship, which is the 'ability of new citizens to participate in society and to engage actively in our democracy' (ibid.). This will help people understand both their 'rights and their obligations as citizens of the UK and strengthen bonds of mutual understanding between people of diverse cultural backgrounds' (ibid.).

Blunkett's approach to integration is based upon the idea of active citizenship, whereby Britishness is largely measured through political participation and involvement in democratic structures. This model of citizenship has been criticised by a number of academics because 'there is an implied process of assimilation or integration which requires more effort on the part of minorities than for white British' (Osler and Starkey 2000:15). Instead, what Osler and Starkey (2000) and Diwan (2008) argue is for the use of the principles of the human rights model within schools as a way of understanding and tackling structural inequalities and discrimination, and also to support young people in developing identities within the context of diversity.

Blair and the duty of integration

Tony Blair (2006) during his time as the Prime Minister of Britain, in his seminal speech on multiculturalism to the Runnymede Trust, chose to define integration through a set of values which attempts to unify people as citizens whilst at the same time excluding others. The London bombers of 7/7, in Blair's understanding, were not integrated into British society despite the fact that all of the perpetrators were born in Britain and had attended state schools. For Blair (2006), integration is defined through a set of British values which cannot be measured through culture or lifestyle choices, but are rather based upon a set of reified British values. Blair (2006) stated:

> When I talk about integration ... It's not about culture or lifestyle. It's about values. It is about integrating at the point of shared,

common unifying British values. It isn't about what defines us as people, but as citizens, the right and duties that go with being a member of our society.

The 'rights and duties' that Blair (2006) chose to use to define the essential values that make someone integrated were the 'belief in democracy, rule of law, tolerance, equal treatment for all, respect for this country and shared heritage'. It is only by buying into these duties that we can claim 'the right to call ourselves British'. Many have identified a sense of irony in this speech, especially given the inclusion of 'rule of law' as one of the central features of Britishness, especially given the questionable legal nature surrounding the British invasion of Iraq. The deliberate use of and rhetorical reference to 'our' society, and also the 'right to call ourselves British', are grounded upon the notions of Britishness predicated upon a set of values that all citizens in general, but *outsider* Muslim communities in particular, had to fully embrace. After all, Blair (2006) argues that 'the right to be in a multicultural society was always implicitly balanced by a duty to integrate'. For Blair (2006), the above-defined values should be asserted within the public realm through set policies; this should also ensure that 'we expect everyone to conform to them'.

Brown, patriotism and a patriotic purpose

During the same year as the Tony Blair speech on integration, the then Deputy Prime Minister Gordon Brown (2006), in his *Fabian New Year Conference* lecture on identity and Britishness almost 11 months prior to Blair's speech on Britishness and integration, focused on the idea of patriotism and patriotic purpose as a way of tackling the issue of integration and the Muslim question. Muslims are required, as a way of integrating into the political community, to demonstrate their allegiance, commitment and patriotism to Britishness, which for Brown (2006) is defined through 'liberty, responsibility and fairness'. For Brown, patriotism is based upon notions of progressive forms of Britishness which is defined through three fundamental values drawn from political philosophy. Brown sees 'British patriotism and patriotic purpose founded on liberty for all, responsibility by all and fairness for all'. For Brown (2006), the political Left needs to embrace the ideas of Britishness and patriotism which for many years had been associated with the political Right; a modern, pro-gressive, forward-looking conceptualisation of Britishness would not equate to a retreat into 'self-interested individualism' but would lead to ideas of 'empowerment'. In the same way, responsibility would not correspond to a 'retreat into a form of paternalism, but is indeed a commitment to the strongest possible civic society'. Finally for Brown (2006), fairness is not simply a formal equality before the law, but is in fact a modern belief in an empowering equality of opportunity for all.

Cameron and muscular liberalism

More recently, Prime Minister David Cameron (2011a) presented his ideas on integration at a security conference in Munich to del-egates of European Union (EU) ministers and heads of state. The speech conflated multiculturalism and integration with security and counter-terrorism policies in a number of ways. First, Cameron made the distinction between 'good' Muslims who see 'Islam as a religion practiced [sic] by people' and 'bad' Muslims who are 'Islamic extrem-ists' who view Islam as a political ideology'. Second, he used the 'slippery slope' argument to draw a link between violent extremism and extremist or illiberal views. This, he argues, is:

> At the furthest end of those who back terrorism to promote their ultimate goal: an entire Islamist realm, governed by an inter-pretation of shariah. Move along the spectrum, and you find people who may reject violence, but who accept various parts of the extremist worldwide, including real hostility towards Western democracy and liberal values.

For Cameron (2011a), one of the main causes of the Muslim prob-lematic is the weakening of collective identity through an emphasis on cultural difference through state multiculturalism which has encouraged an idea of separateness, and for cultures to have paral-lel existences distanced not only from each other but also from the mainstream. In the past, Cameron (2011a) argued that these forms of cultural-segregation, which he feels run in contrast to British main-stream society, have been tolerated and encouraged by the state. The failure, according to Cameron (2011a), has been the state's reluctance to provide a robust vision of a society to which Muslims would 'want to feel they want to belong'. A potential way forward in addressing the Muslim question is through the idea of 'muscular liberalism'. Although Cameron (2011a) did not define what he meant by muscular liberalism, his choice of a strong rhetorical vocabulary provides an insight into the hard-line approach to 'tolerance' of cultural difference in general and state-funded practices of multiculturalism in particular. Cameron argues that 'frankly, we need a lot less of the passive tolerance of recent years and a much more active, muscular liberalism'. Moreover, Cameron argues that belonging to the state is to believe in the principles of liberalism which are based on 'freedom of speech, democracy, rule of law and equal rights of race, sex or sexuality'. In short, 'muscular liberalism' focuses less on the hitherto practices of liberalism of passive tolerance, rather it puts greater emphasis on an assertive and bold liberalism which actively defends and pursues the principles of secular liberalism. More recently, Cameron (2014) responding to the Trojan Horse saga and the question of self-segregation by drawing upon the language and style of 'muscular liberalism' as a way of framing the Trojan Horse controversy, arguing that all schools as a matter of principle should have to promote Britishness and British values. The ironic twist in discourse of British values comes at a time when David Cameron is promising to take Britain out of the European Convention for Human Rights (Holehouse 2014), especially given the history and the British involvement in drafting of the articles of European Convention on Human Rights (McNally 2010).

Shared values or enforced values

There are a number of problems associated with the way integration or the question of segregation is framed by Blair (2006), Brown (2006) and Cameron (2011a). First, the idea of Britishness and integration is linked to the discourse of values as an oppositional positioning for the Muslim problematic. Whilst there are subtle nuances in the above approaches to shared values, a certain moral panic can nevertheless be seen to have been generated through the essentialised Muslim presence. Second, there are also a number of fundamental flaws in the way in which shared values are conceptualised and, especially given the starting premise of the debate, it is difficult to see how the values discussed by the above political actors are 'shared values'; rather, it is clear from the style and content of the debate that these are essentially values enforced by a politically dominant class on a powerless minority group. Third, the theoretical positioning of shared values as noted above is grounded on an 'absolutist position', which is based upon the dominant values of the host society (Leicester 1989). This position can be contrasted with a 'cultural relativist' approach which sees the 'shared values' approach as difficult or at least impossible to achieve, as it is socially and culturally defined. In order to provide an exit between the 'absolutist' and 'cultural relativist' approach, a 'limited relativist' position can be used for an inclusive political project, which views shared values as a collective project that is ongoing and negotiated by all concerned (ibid.). Finally, integration as 'shared values' approaches views Islam through an orientalist lens – Islam is essentially different from Western secular mores and it's only through adopting an enlightened Western secular worldview that Muslims can have a future in the West. Moreover, the political speeches by Blair (2006), Brown (2006) and Cameron (2010a) carry an implicit approach to either relegating Muslim behaviour to the private sphere or sanitising Islam, so that it accepts the neo-liberal secular consensus.

Integration as political rhetoric

Integration, assimilation and acculturation are all idioms that are frequently used interchangeably within the public discourse. The integration debate within a tense political climate, especially given the ongoing War on Terror, is best understood not as ongoing process whereby minority communities gradually adopt the values and norms of British society, neither is it framed within the principles of multiculturalism that aims to promote cultural pluralism and cultural diversity which recognises different ways of participating in Britishness. Rather, as will be argued, the understanding of integration juxtaposes the security agenda with cultural assault on Muslim values through an oppositional discourse.

Contemporary framing of self-segregation through the political rhetoric of integration is best understood through a detailed analysis of the variety of ways in which it plays as a reified normative construct, aimed at achieving certain socio-political objectives. Integration, in light of the security agenda, is seen as a highly politicised construct which is riddled with paradoxes, politically motivated self-interests and above all as being based on questionable empirical evidence.

The idea of integration implies an objective towards socio-political equilibrium in society between the host society and the 'new' community, this equilibrium being particularly pertinent given national and the international security concerns with the 'Islamist threat'. Most of this public discourse is based more on the fear of the 'other' rather than on any given reality. Moreover, given the absence of any evidence which draws links between high levels of segregation and violent extremism, it is important for academics 'to cast a suspicious eye on any claim that the social world operates in an orderly way and with a tendency towards equilibrium' (Bauman and Testler 2001:11). A useful theoretical framework for understanding the discourse of integration and its association with modernity is to view the main objective of modern nation states, particularly during a tense political atmosphere, as being to maintain public order in society; this order is achieved by ensuring that all migrant communities are fully assimilated into the dominant culture of the nation state. The process of so doing creates a sense of 'otherness' in those who do not fit in. By using the Jewish experience of pre-war Germany, the sociologist Zymunt Bauman (1991) highlights how assimilation can lead to a sense of contradiction, spiritual isolation and loneliness and, most importantly, a feeling of ambivalence. Moreover, he demonstrates this by drawing parallels with the Jewish experience, and how they were identified as having a 'problematic presence' in a number of Western European societies in the twentieth century (Bauman and Tester 2001). The following outlook, which is summarised below, can be used to understand how, within the contemporary context, a similar sense of ambivalence is ascribed to Muslims through misrepresentation and categorisation as 'pariahs' (Santios 2004).

> Acculturation did not incorporate the Jews into German society, but transformed them into a separate, ambivalent and incongruous, non-category category of 'assimilated Jews', prised from the traditional Jewish community as much as from native German elites... The assimilating Jews acted under the pressure to prove their German-hood, yet the very attempt to prove it was held against them as the evidence of their duplicity and, in all probability, also of subversive intentions.
>
> (Bauman 1991:120–121)

Contemporary educational policy relating to race and religion often uses the discourses on integration and Britishness through a series of liberal hegemonic positioning to reinforce a sense of moral hierarchy. These ideas are often politically motivated and hermeneutically loaded concept which is used to mean 'assimilation' (Back et al. 2002; Kalra and Kapoor 2008). The interchangeable use of integration and assimilation following the July 2005 London bombings is aimed at nurturing a sense of *aggressive majoritarianism* – this occurs when 'majority dislike and prejudice towards Muslims are enforced in the name of common sense, integration and even security' (Gilborn 2008:81). In short, the function of integration, within the context of education, is a mechanism of *governmentality* (Ball 2013) that is used to control and manage Muslim behaviour through the function of power which is embedded not only in discourse but also in policy. The concept of governmentality was initially developed by the French philosopher Michel Foucault (Burchell et al. 1991), which in general terms, refers to 'any relatively calculated practice to direct categories of social agent to specified ends [by] plurality of agencies and authorities, of aspects of behaviour to be governed' (Dean 1991, cited in Ball 2013:120).

Integration: policy of undermining integration

The political debate on integration is a political construct that is used by politicians and endorsed by the media to refer to minority communities in general and Muslim communities in particular. The concept of Britishness does little to function as a public policy; it does little to create or shed any insights, but rather is a tool designed to be used to keep Muslims in check. Thus integration and Britishness is far from being a process or transition which minority communities undergo over a period of time, but rather is a concept which can be interrogated in order to make sense of the ways in which Muslim communities are framed.

For Muslims the problem of 'integration' does not exist as a 'problem' because cultural change is a natural and inevitable process for most minority communities. Thus the consequences arising from the racialised discourses of integration does not serve the interests of minority communities; the objective of this discourse is neither to encourage nor to motivate Muslims to be active citizens but rather to continue to demonise and essentialise Muslim communities in

Britain. This is clearly demonstrated in the following observation made by a Muslim activist with a long track record of working in the field of race equality. It shows how the major theme arising from the above debate on integration, Britishness and shared values is that it is a political tool used to 'beat' Muslims into place:

> Like I say, the term integration is used to stir up racial hatred and really it is a term that is used by the media and the political class to BEAT people with. Integration is a very good story for the press because it has become a noted issue. If you look at integration the automatic thing that comes to your mind is Islam and the way in which people dress. So I would say that integration is a big problem.

As will be made clear in this book, Muslim communities do not have a major problem with integration; the problem rather lies in the politicisation and racialisation of the concept, because the debate on integration amongst politicians is understood as its oppositional stance by Islam and Muslims. It connects to a wider debate on how Britain or even Europe is imagined; for many Islam in Europe it acts as *transruption* to the Judeo-Christian secular heritage. The function of Islamophobia in Europe 'stems from the defence and resistance against the possible effects of real multicultural contacts between Islamic values and European – Western ones' (Marranci 2004:105). The conceptualisation of integration sees Islam as a socio-political threat to Western secular values; it consists of 'any series of contestory cultural and theoretical interventions which, in their impact as cultural differences, unsettle social norms and threaten to dismantle hegemonic concepts and practices' (Hesse 2000:17). The idea of transruption is evident in the public debate in some Western European countries with a traditional history of cultural tolerance, over the visible signs of Islam in public spaces. For example, the growing public concern in Switzerland translated into a vote to ban the construction of new minarets. The move was brought about by the Swiss People's Party, which capitalised on the broader discussion on Muslim integration and the visible displays of segregation in Switzerland and collected 100,000 signatures from voters backing the motion for a referendum; which saw almost 60 per cent of the Swiss population and 22 out of the 26 states favouring a ban on minarets (Ammann 2009).

In recent months much as been said about the nature of British society, including the intervention of the Prime Minister declaring that Britain is fundamentally a Christian country. In announcing 'a committed but I have to say vaguely practicing [sic] – Church of England Christian, who will stand up for the values and principles of my faith' at Oxford during the 400th anniversary of the King James Bible, Cameron (2011b) called for a revival of traditional Christian values to counter Britain's 'moral collapse'. Using assertive language, Cameron (2011b) stressed that 'We are a Christian country and we should not be afraid to say so', and that 'live and let live' had too often been associated with 'do what you please'. More crucially, the framing of the British values discourse was done through the Christian perspective by arguing how not only 'our language, culture and politics is steeped in the Christian Bible' but also 'human rights and equality to our constitutional monarchy and parliamentary democracy'. He further added how 'from the role of the church in the first forms of welfare provision, to the many modern-day, faith-led social action projects...the Bible has been a spur to action for people of faith throughout history, and it remains so today'. To use the 400th anniversary of the King James Bible to talk about how 'we' are living in a Christian country, especially given the history of the King James Bible and its contextual backdrop of struggles between Catholicism and the Church of England, means that the framing of a 'Christian country' takes on a meta-narrative of the history and politics linked with the Church of England. To reinforce the idea of a 'Christian Country', the then Education Secretary, Michael Gove, planned to distribute a leather-bound copy of the King James Bible, written in seventeenth-century English, to every state primary and secondary school in the country (Vasagar 2013).

Integration, historical memory in shaping prejudice

The Muslim community discourse draws upon the historical treatment of other minority groups in the UK, particularly the treatment of Jewish, Irish and Black immigrant communities. The current political rhetoric against the Muslim community was seen as a manifestation of historical forms of prejudice experienced by other minority communities (Curtis 1968, 1997; Bhatcharyya 2008; Meer 2010). Integration has always been a 'hot political' issue; in fact, the idea of integration as a political tool has a long socio-cultural history. This has been highlighted by a number of academic studies covering the extensive literature of anti-Semitism, racism and anti-Irish prejudice (Curtis 1968, 1997; Hall et al. 1978; Frankel and Zipperstein 1992; Gilroy 1987). More particularly, there are parallels with how the concept of integration in the context of the Jewish experience in the nineteenth century focused on the question of Jewish loyalty to Jerusalem; or how the question of loyalty towards the Irish question was framed around the Pope or the nation state. In the same way, the contemporary question of Muslim loyalty is framed around the question of loyalty towards values of Britishness over the values of the 'Muslim ummah'. The *Tebbit test* is an expression that has been often used to test the question of loyalty. The Tebbit test was developed by the Conservative politician, Sir Norman Tebbit, in April 1990. Tebbit suggested that immigrant communities in Britain should have strong loyalty to the country to which they had migrated and not to the country they had left. Tebbit used the analogy of cricket, particularly looking at which side is supported by immigrant communities, as a way of measuring loyalty. He further argued that a large proportion of British Muslims would fail to pass this test (Carvel 2004). Whilst this statement was made in an interview with the *Los Angeles Times* as early as 1990, the Tebbit test has often been cited by the political Right as a litmus test which would have prevented the London bombings had the authorities taken heed of Tebbit's policies on assimilation.

The history of anti-terrorist legislation, especially that used against Irish dissidents wrongly convicted of IRA terrorism such as the Guildford Four, was cited as experience within the parental discourse in order to draw parallels between the current situation of Muslims and past experiences of the Irish community. The high-profile lawyer and human rights activist Gareth Pierce, who defended the Birmingham Six, Guildford Four and leading Muslim suspects charged with terrorism, including the Guantanamo inmate Moazzam Begg (2006), has played a crucial part in placing the 'Muslim struggle' within the broader Irish experience (Begg 2013). The current Muslim experience of anti-Muslim prejudice and also the wider questions about Britishness, integration and self-segregation can be located within a continuum of old forms of hatred, such as anti-Irish and anti-Semitism. Having said that, there are certain unique features as far as the Muslim problem is concerned; the reason for this is sum-marised by the following narrative. It demonstrates how the sheer size of the Muslim population, combined with 24-hour news broad-casting, means that the attention focused on the Muslim community takes an unprecedented form.

> Integration has always been a hot political issue, if you look back at history you will find that it has always been a political issue, because whenever you have had large-scale migration into UK by people coming from overseas to settle in any given land whether this be UK or many other countries you will have cultural clashes. You will also get a set of myths that will contribute towards those clashes. You will have myths that will generate hate, whether they are the myths of the Jews sacrificing the children of the Christians which is a famous myth that grew and which was used to persecute the Jews. Or if it's the myth around the modern age around Islam advocating the forced marriage of women. So these are myths that can be used to whip up fear or strife or social tensions. The reason why we have so many myths around Islam and Muslims today compared with the past I would say is the prevalent nature of the mass media and also introduction of various new media.

It is clear that the questions regarding integration, loyalty and seg-regation are located not only within a broader historical context that includes similar myths or moral panics that have been used to generate hate against minority communities. The above exam-ple demonstrates how integration is used by political and media sources as a way of talking about minority groups, and these ways of posing or framing particular questions are often recycled through-out history (Cohen 1980; Alexander 2000). The above experiences of anti-Muslim prejudice (Malik 2009) in the form of political and media discourses (McCreary et al. 2007) are seen as an important factor shaping the Muslim view of integration. The current tensions around Islam in the UK, following the events of 9/11 and 7/7, have deeply politicised the Muslim community and have further under-mined the Muslim position on integration; some parents felt they have been being 'pushed' into a corner and forced to take a *stance*. Taking a stance requires an active role, which nurtures the collective Muslim solidarity to respond to external political events, and this often requires them to take an opposite position to that of the status quo. The observations, highlighted below, provide a clear account of the way in which political debates on integration are dismissed and resisted, based upon a wider framework of social acceptance and rejection. One of the key comparisons offered by a number of Muslim respondents focused on the importance of maintaining and nurturing one's cultural identity and maintaining the spirit of group solidarity.

Well the obvious question is 7/7 and 9/11, people have been pushed to one corner – you will find that people have been forced to take side and take a stance. People need a common enemy; today the Muslims fit that bill. You have to act against your enemy, when the government does something against the common enemy it makes you feel safe and secure – well that's been a part of it. When we look at stop and search we know that certain communities are targeted by the authorities.

[And]:

> You see I am sick and tired of the way in which the government is lecturing us on integration; take Cameron's recent speech on multiculturalism, integration and Britishness. I have one thing for Cameron – he can shove his liberalism up his backside. I am sick to death, I have realised one thing even if we all became liberals overnight, if we all went to the pub for a swift half. They will still call us a Paki bastard. So I might as well be a Paki with principle. One thing that I know for sure if you stick to who you are, you will get respect at the end.

The wider political rhetoric on integration was considered by many Muslims to be one-dimensional. It involves the government in general and the media in particular 'telling' the Muslim community to integrate. This one-dimensional debate on integration does not provide a space for Muslims to convey apprehensions or concerns they may have over certain practices within the wider society. Respondents felt there was no room for the Muslim community to participate in the debate on integration; any genuine criticism of certain experiences is discredited in the name of 'segregation' and 'disloyalty'. The following respondent argues the need for a debate on integration based upon a negotiated debate on shared values.

A negotiated approach to shared values sees social values not as an absolutist dominant set of majoritarian values but as a collective and inclusive negotiated activity (Haydon 2008; Leicester 1989; Halstead 2009).

Shared values seem to be in fashion as far as the debate of integration is concerned. I see this discussion to be problematic, it does not help anything. I have been in this country long enough to realise that this discussion is a non-starter. My socialist friends in our trade union will object to Cameron's set of values. So let's not have a set of values which are pushed on us, instead let's have a mature debate about these values and try and mutually agree on these values.

Integration and the question of acceptance

The Black Muslim convert perspective on the question of recognition, acceptance and dignity provides an insight into the way integration is understood and framed. The majority of the Muslim communities in UK consist of the dominant South Asian ethnic cohort. Recently, following the events of 9/11 and 7/7, the convert community in general and the Black convert Muslim community in particular have been a focal point in the media debate. The role of Jermaine Lindsay, one of the 7/7 bombers, and Richard Reid, the shoe bomber, together with the active role played by the Brixton Mosque in combating extremism, have placed the Black Muslim convert community in the national spotlight (Reedie 2009). The broader appeal of the Black Muslim aesthetic within the 'Hip Hop' industry (Miah and Kalra 2008), combined with the growing academic literature articulating a Black-American cultural experience of Islam (Jackson 2005), have contributed to the importance of studying the Black Muslim convert community in the UK (Reddie 2009). In addition, unlike the White Muslim convert respondents, the Black convert experience provided a distinctive cultural reading of integration within the context of the *Windrush* experience. The convert discourse focused primarily on racism, and the way in which the White host society failed to accept a Black Christian community travelling to the 'motherland'. This was partly to do with the way in which the notion of Britishness and integration is framed within normative construct Whiteness, but also with the fundamental issue of acceptance. This is an important issue because it places the question of ownership not only on the migrant communities but also on the host society and asks the crucial question of whether or not Muslim will be fully accepted within the construct of Britishness, or whether the fundamental definition of Britishness is antithetical to Muslims, as noted below by a Muslim parent and community activist in Manchester:

> At the end of the day it's all about understanding, when our parents first came here on the *Windrush*, there were a lot of concerns about 'these' foreigners who came in on the *Windrush*. Our community faced a great deal of hostility, despite the fact that they were Christians travelling to the motherland. This continued when we went to school, we realised that all the minority communities had the same difficulty with racism and harassment. We also realised that it wasn't only the racist kids in the school that was giving us grief it was the system. We realised that it was the government that run the system and it was almost that they were stoking up fears of Black men that created a culture of resentment.

Christianity, together with a broader conceptualisation of Britishness, was not sufficient for the *Windrush* community to be socially accepted, and in many respects the ideas advocated by Cameron (2011b) in regard to Britain being a Christian country are perceived through perspectives of Whiteness that not only exclude Muslims but also other Christians who do not conform to the Church of England outlook on Christianity. This further motivated many Black community members to establish Black churches in the UK (Reddie 2009). The reason behind this development, as pointed out by one of the respondents, was 'not because they wanted to display signs of self-segregation' but rather as a consequence of the 'rejection by the mainstream host community'. Black convert responses developed their narratives of integration by drawing upon the above *Windrush* experiences to shape their understanding of integration. Many argued that they were in a privileged position to articulate a nuanced Muslim perspective on integration, and this is clearly articulated as follows:

> You see we are quite lucky because we were born Christians but decided to convert or revert to Islam. When people talk about integration we know it's a joke. After all we were Christians and spoke

English even our names were anglicised. But despite all this integration where did it get us! You see at the end of the day even if
you behaved like the average white man – to them you are still
an outsider. You will still get stopped in the street by the police.
So I say you can keep your integration we know it's a joke.

The convert perspectives on integration show how, despite attempting to integrate into British society, they were left with a feeling of
rejection and isolation. Many argued that the question of integration
should not be whether 'Muslims were willing to integrate into British
society' but whether there is a 'willingness to accept Muslims as
British citizens'. The following observation provides a clear account
of the way in which political debates on integration are dismissed
and resisted, based upon a wider framework of social acceptance
and rejection. One of the key comparisons offered by a number of
Muslim respondents focused on the importance of maintaining and
nurturing one's cultural identity and maintaining the spirit of group
identity. This is further articulated by the following example, which
drew upon some of the paradoxes of integration:

> You have to realise that we can never all be the same, you see
> Michael Jackson tried changing his colour to white. My question
> is, did that earn him more or less respect by the white community?
> The answer is less. The point is this when he was Black he was
> not accepted and even when he changed is colour he wasn't. He
> should have realised that his fans liked him for what he was that
> was his music. So staying true to who you are is very important.
> There is no point changing for the political masters. At work there
> is this guy that likes to go to the pub, he likes to stay away from
> the Muslims or the Asian community. He thinks that this will get
> him more respect. At the end of the day people should respect you
> and accept you for who you are. I won't change for no-one.

Conclusion

By analysing the role of 'race' and ethnicity in policy discourse,
we are able to trace a dynamic and often complex link between
issues of racism and key policy pronouncements. We are able
to critically deconstruct policies that claim (often explicitly)

to be unconnected with 'race' whilst simultaneously granting legitimacy to a particular racist definition of 'us' (the 'real' British, the heart of the nation) as opposed to 'them' (outsiders – such as 'alien' ethnic minorities – and the enemies within).

(Gilborn 1995:20)

The above observation provides a summary of an account that has articulated the intricate relationship between the questions of race, racism and educational policy and practice. Whilst the above quote is taken from Gilborn's early research on racism and schools, it nevertheless captures the current sentiments surrounding Muslims and educational policy by highlighting the way in which racialised discourse is produced and reproduced over a period of time by the state. In light of the ideas of the racial state (Goldberg 2002), it does not come as a surprise that following the events of 7/7 and the Trojan Horse debate, British Muslims continue to be governed through policy discourses around Britishness and shared values.

The policy framing of integration as demonstrated above is presented as being diametrically opposite to the West. The former is often projected as obscurantist, undemocratic and misogynistic, whilst the latter is seen as secular, advanced and grounded upon the principles of liberalism. This binary discourse not only leads to further marginalisation of British Muslim communities but also towards policies which are deeply counterproductive. Whilst this type of reasoning has gained particular momentum following the events of 9/11 and 7/7, the ideological antecedents have a long intellectual and historical tradition. These can be traced back to the eighth century with the rise of Islam as a dominant political force (Said 1978/1997; Djait 1985; Daniel 1991; Macfie 2000). This form of Manichean framing of the 'other' as usually diametrically opposite to the civilised West has colonial antecedents. The framing of the 'other' thus becomes a product of Western ideological biases articulated through scholarship and systems of thought (Said 1978). The current treatment of Muslims can be seen not only as a continuation of the colonial legacy, but also as part of the racialised political treatment (Goldberg 2002) of minority communities in Britain.

The increasing Muslim presence in Europe, together with the growing security concerns about Muslim communities, in recent years, has given rise to this discursive framing of the Muslim problematic, which is often associated with anti-Muslim racism (Kundnani 2007) and Islamophobia (Marranci 2004; Allen 2010). Anti-Muslim racism and Islamophobia are dominant approaches which have attempted to make sense of the current discourse on self-segregation within a wider context of 'new racism' (Barker 1981). The concept of anti-Muslim racism is used to explain the phenomenon of 'new racism', which focuses less on the hostility against Islam and more on the aggression and prejudice against Muslims – that is to say anti-Muslim prejudice focuses on the 'lives of Muslims' in the West (Malik 2009).

The contemporary discourses on 'integrationism' are seen to be a response to the political culture associated with the War on Terror, self-segregation and alien values (Kundnani 2007). The politics of integration has played an instrumental role in creating levels of *moral panics* at a global level (Morgan and Poynting 2012), which has often been justified on the grounds of 'legitimate concerns' of extremist threat or the act of undermining principles of secular liberalism. The idea of integration then becomes a parallel feature of the War on Terror aimed at managing Muslim cultural practices which are seen to represent a 'threat' to Europe from within, with their adherence to Muslim values, norms and presence which threatens the notion of European-ness itself (Fekete 2009).

The socio-political context through which the debate of self-segregation is debated has had significant impact on different ways in which Muslim pupils experience anti-Muslim racism through schooling; research on Muslim pupils' experience of schooling has demonstrated how the concept of integration can be used as a tool to criticise Muslim pupils for not mixing with their white peers and failing to attend school trips or participating in extracurricular activities – even though these actions were motivated by a complex set of factors including acceptance of anti-Muslim prejudice and racial harassment by both staff and pupils (Crozier and Davies 2008).

3
Educational Policy and Muslim Self-Segregation

> The failure to fully integrate Muslims within the societies of France, Germany and the United Kingdom has the potential to foster social and political instability in those states over both the short and long terms.
>
> (Pauley 2004:4)

> Aggressive majoritarianism...the rights and perspectives of the White majority were now asserted, sometimes in the name of 'integration' and 'cohesion' (code words for contemporary assimilation) but also simply on the basis that the majority disliked certain things (such as Muslim veils) and now felt able to enforce those prejudices in the name of common sense, integration and even security.
>
> (Gilborn 2008:81)

The self-segregation thesis has become a dominant discourse shaping Muslim geographical space within the UK and also within a range of other European countries such as France (Bowen 2007; Laborde 2008). Segregation is often seen through the lenses of the 2001 race riots and the events of 9/11 and 7/7 and, as a result, the segregated nature of some European cities is seen by many political actors as highly problematic, from the perspective of both social disorder and radical extremism. The problem of self-segregation, especially in light of the Trojan Horse saga in Birmingham, is seen to be a key feature in debating the question of loyalty in British society, which is ultimately linked to social and religious conservatism vis-à-vis the notion that Muslims prefer to give loyalty to their religion and 'ummah' over nation state and secular liberal space.

The ongoing debates on self-segregation that have arisen have raised a number of policy questions regarding self-segregation of Muslim communities. For some, these concerns are part of an emerging threat that requires urgent and radical public policy interventions (Philips 2005) whilst for others, such debates on self-segregation are politically constructed moral panics which lack detailed empirical evidence (Finney and Simpson 2009).

It has been shown how international events regarding Muslim communities have helped shape their worldview primarily through socio-political and religious lenses. In fact, more recent events in Syria with the involvement of British Muslim fighters have further questioned the idea of loyalty to the Muslim ummah over loyalty to the nation state. Ideas associated with cultural self-segregation also includes notions of political segregation, in that growing numbers of Muslims are not happy with the current political structure of liberal democracy and want to replace it with a narrow religious theocracy based upon the principles of Islamic State. Discourses over political segregation are informed by the events unfolding in Syria and Iraq (Cockburn 2015). The recent promotional and recruitment video by Islamic State in Iraq and Levant (ISIS), watched by thousands of people in Britain, dominated much of the headlines of most of the British press showing three British Muslims – Reyaad Khan with fellow school friend Nasser Muthana, from Cardiff, and a third man named as Abdul Raqib Amin, from Aberdeen – has caused much concern over the radicalisation of Muslim youths in Britain as a result of the Syrian civil war. It is estimated that up to 400 British fighters may be fighting in Syria against the forces of Bashir al-Asad (Townsend 2014). Moreover, it is argued that some of these are fighting for the radical organisation ISIS, whose stated objective is not only to overthrow Asad's regime in Syria but also to implement Islamic State. More recently, ISIS has taken control of a number of strategic locations in Iraq, has self-declared certain parts of that country as Islamic State and nominated their leader Bakr al-Baghdadi as its caliph. Whilst the implications of British Muslim fighters who have pledged allegiance to ISIS, have been questioned by a number of researchers, they argue that much of the evidence shows that most foreign fighters have remained in Syria (Bew and Mayer 2014). Nevertheless, a concern around Muslim cultural and political self-segregation continues to be a critical feature in education and broader public policy. In fact, the debates around the Trojan Horse and the embedding of the Prevent Strategy within schools demonstrate how international events help shape local issues and concerns.

This chapter will highlight the significant shift in educational discourse of Muslim communities in Britain; it builds on the discussion in the previous chapter of framing Muslims by highlighting how the question of self-segregation is dealt with in educational policy. It is worthwhile to note these developments in both priority and emphasis have changed the direction of British race relations policies away from a focus on race to one on religion, ethnicity and culture. In attempting to deal with some of the many issues arising from the security questions, the British government juxtaposed counter-terrorism measures with a range of policy reports dating back to the 2001 riots in the north of England, which hitherto have captured the public's 'concerns' over segregated communities in general and non-White monocultural schools in particular. This chapter intends to build on the discussions highlighted above by providing a detailed analysis of contemporary thinking on education and integration with particular regard to Muslim communities. This chapter provides a detailed analysis of the New Labour policy of using school academies, which was continued under the coalition government between the Conservative and Liberal Democrat parties to tackle self-segregation in order to prevent violent extremism.

The Trojan Horse effect: tackling cultural self-segregation through inspection

The question of segregation within state schools in England is seen as a major social problem which if left unchallenged could lead to outbreak of social disorder or, at worst, to violent extremism. These concerns over self-segregation within state schools were openly debated within the context of the Ofsted inspection of schools connected to the Trojan Horse stories. It was argued by Sir Michael Wilshaw (2014), Ofsted's chief inspector, that Muslim children in state schools needed an understanding and appreciation of other cultures and communities. One of the ways through which this would be achieved in the future was by empowering Ofsted inspectors to use the inspection framework to ensure that schools would be teaching a balanced curriculum. In fact, Ofsted have had these powers since the previous New Labour government introduced the Education Inspection Act in 2006, which placed a duty on all maintained schools to promote community cohesion as part of their Ofsted inspection process (DSCF 2007). The Ofsted inspection framework 2014 continues to focus on community cohesion as part of a broader collective inspection of the spiritual, moral, social and cultural (SMSC) development of children (Ofsted 2014).

In light of the Trojan Horse stories it is clear that the question of segregation would become a crucial feature in regard to inspection, particularly for state schools with a high proportion of Muslim pupils. First, the social political context and the focus on segregation and Muslim communities means that there may be inconsistency in the way that SMSC is used disproportionally in regard to states schools with Muslim pupils. Second, it is clear from the assessment of the 21 school inspection reports from Birmingham (see Chapter 1) that the Prevent agenda was a significant feature of all the schools inspected (Miah 2014) – despite the acceptance by Sir Michael Wilshaw in response to questions from the Education Select Committee that Ofsted did not find any evidence of students being radicalised at school (House of Commons 2014). This sets a precedent for schools within the same socio-cultural profile to be assessed through the Prevent lens, and is not an over-exaggeration especially given that the Trojan Horse stories have been followed up by Ofsted inspectors in areas with a high proportion of Muslim communities, such as Bradford, London and Luton. Third, given the moral panic over Muslims and self-segregation, it appears that any future inspection of schools in those particular areas could lead to that inspection being biased. Finally, as noted in the Education Select Committee's interview with Sir Michael Wilshaw, the lack of clarity surrounding key terms such as 'secular state schools', 'extremism' and the role of multiculturalism in state schools would mean that inspection of Muslim schools would be politically defined (ibid.).

Tackling self-segregation as a de-radicalisation imperative

Following the 7 July bombing, British Muslims have increasingly been seen through a set of pathological lenses, and Muslim neighbourhoods have been viewed as 'ghettos' which are hotbeds of terrorism. In response to these events, government discourse has had a tendency to read the overarching political events through the prisms of segregation and integration of Muslim communities.

One of the key ways of tackling the question of self-segregation has been the 'community relations' approach to de-radicalisation, which 'examines the central problematic associated with presenting Muslim communities as suspect communities in the "war on terror"' (McGee 2008:8). Part of this 'community relations' approach incorporates the notion of ethnic spatial segregation resulting in racial conflict and cultural self-segregation and leading on to a slippery slope towards violent extremism. The extension of community cohesion to national security, within the context of the educational system, is a theme that can be identified in the Department for Children, Schools and Families' prevention of violent extremism toolkit, titled *Learning Together to Be Safe*. This toolkit blurs the parameters between teaching and de-radicalisation by allowing counter-terrorism to enter the domain of teaching. More significantly, the 'advice' and 'guidance' outlined within this toolkit to schools uses a range of approaches which compromise the integrity and transparency of teacher–pupil relations by including the police and counter-terror officials in the sharing of information on potential Al-Qaeda-related activities. One of the more high-profile cases that attracted national attention involved a nine-year-old schoolboy in east London allegedly showing 'signs of extremism' (Dodd 2009).

The coalition-led government's revised Prevent Strategy (HM Government 2011), instead of abandoning this highly critical approach to counter-terrorism, which had attracted considerable public backlash (Kundnani 2009; House of Commons 2010) for its possible human rights infringements given that young students had been referred to the police for expressing controversial opinions, was given further support both financially and through greater strategic collaboration between the Department of Education (DoE) and the Office for Security and Counter-Terrorism (OSCT). Furthermore, the revised Prevent Strategy (HM Government 2011) also placed the Channel

Project, the government's multi-agency risk management initiative, in a role in the fight against terror by integrating this within the government's child protection and safeguarding policies. The Channel Project has come under great scrutiny, especially through the Preventing Violence Extremism Select Committee, on the grounds of its possible human rights infringements given that some young students are referred to the police for expressing controversial opinions which may, technically, be within the law. The blurring of the boundaries between what is legal and what is illegal vis-à-vis the debate on violent extremism and political or cultural forms of extremism, in addition to the policy implications of the Prevent policy, is succinctly summarised below.

> There is strong evidence that a significant part of the Prevent programme involves the embedding of counter-terrorism police officers within the delivery of local services, the purpose of which seems to be to gather intelligence on Muslim communities, to identify areas, groups and individuals that are 'at risk' and to then facilitate interventions, such as the Channel programme.
>
> (Kundnani 2009:6)

Consolidation between the national security agenda, integration policies and the schooling nexus is visible in works of Sir Cyril Taylor. Taylor was a key figure within both the Conservative and New Labour educational hierarchy, this being clear from fact that he served as an advisor to ten successive secretaries of Education from the Thatcher era to 2007. For Taylor (2009), it is the Muslim community, as compared with other groups, which displays a problematic presence for the national security agenda. Part of this problem lies in the inability of Muslims to assimilate. The failure to 'assimilate', which Taylor uses interchangeably with 'integrate', can allow extremist world views based on violent radical Islamism to fester; and, more significantly, if such behaviours are not governed this could lead to greater racial and religious violence. Such a picture of complete anomie with increasing levels of criminal and antisocial behaviour would ultimately lead to lawlessness. Instead, what needs to happen to prevent such dystopia is to better integrate Muslim communities. This idea of integration, used as a tool for governance, then becomes an essential feature of school policies. Taylor (2009) argues that Muslims can be integrated into mainstream society through the School Academies programme, and the reason for his opinion is grounded in a de-radicalisation imperative which is summarised in the following interview.

> Our Muslim communities are much more likely to help the police over atrocities such as the July 7 tube bombings if they are better integrated. It is a radical step but I believe a multi-faith community academy initiative can create new schools in socially deprived areas with a far more balanced intake of pupils.
>
> (Taylor, in Garner 2007)

The *spatial narrative* effect: tacking self-segregation through ethnically 'mixed schools'.

An assessment of four local authority areas in the north of England demonstrates how some local authorities have used the programme of rebuilding new schools as a way of tackling the issue of school segregation by merging schools with different ethnic cohorts. This approach to desegregation typically involves a school with a mainly Muslim cohort merging with another with a predominantly White intake. Table 3.1 provides examples of four local authorities in the north of England that have adopted such an approach. Whilst the schools highlighted below are not the only local authorities to have adopted such radical measures to govern Muslim communities through integration policies, nevertheless they provide a better insight into the impacts of school desegregation. It is critical to note that these four local authorities that adopted such a measure have not been selected randomly; all four areas in question have witnessed excessive media coverage of their Muslim communities, which has given way to particular *spatial narratives* of Muslim geographical space. Blackburn dominated the media spotlight following Jack Straw's (2006) comment piece for the local *Lancashire Telegraph* on the *niqab controversy*; the article generated a national debate on whether Muslim women should wear the face veil in public spaces. Following the London bombings, Leeds was suddenly subjected to international media attention after it was identified that three of the four 7/7 bombers were from that city; in fact two of them, Mohammad Siddique Khan and Hasib Hussain, were alumni of Matthew Murray High School in Holbeck, Leeds – which was one of the schools involved in the school merger (see Table 3.1). Burnley and Oldham,

Table 3.1   School academies and ethnically 'mixed schools'

Local authority	Schools with significant Muslim school cohort	School merger with mainly White school cohort	New school created from merger
Blackburn with Darwen	Beardwood High School	Pupils dispersed throughout borough	–
Burnley	Ivy Bank School	Habegam School	Hameldon Community College
Leeds	Matthew Murray High School	Merlyn Rees Community High	South Leeds Academy
Oldham	Grange School	Relocation	Oldham Academy North
Oldham	Kaskenmoor Secondary School	South Chadderton School	Oasis Academy
Oldham	Breeze Hill School	Counthill School	Waterhead Academy

both of which experienced the 2001 summer riots, initially instigated the debates on integration and segregation.

An assessment of the schools programme adopted by the local authorities established the following structural attempts at desegregation. Schools with a predominant or increasing Muslim student population were either (a) closed and merged with schools having a predominantly White cohort or (b) closed, and the pupils were dispersed to neighbouring schools throughout the borough. Consequently school mergers changed the school boundaries and therefore limited the problem previously caused by the existence of monocultural primary feeder schools, opening up new schools to a broader geographic boundary. More crucially, the physical location of new buildings arising from these mergers was most often in mainly White residential areas. It is important to note that establishment of all the schools highlighted below was strongly resisted by the local White communities (Miah 2012) and, in the case of two of the schools (Leeds and Burnley), these were to experience 'bitter warfare' (Hutchinson and Rosser 2005) with 'rising levels of racial tensions' (Rosser 2005), which culminated in 'full-scale riots' (Murphy 2008).

Mixed schools, social contact and group dynamics

Ideas associated with ethnically mixed school have a long and complicated history in regard to sociology or even the philosophy of education. Some of the early advocates of 'common schooling' can be traced back to the works of the American educationalist John Dewey (1916), some 40 years before the landmark Supreme Court case ruling – Brown v. Board of Education (1954), which declared racially segregated schools in the US unconstitutional (Bell 2004). The 'common school' sees the objective of schooling as a process which nurtures a common purpose or an outlook for a better future A fundamental feature that allows this to take place is the sharing of common space which encourages communication between pupils – communication is seen as 'a process of sharing experiences till it becomes a common position' (Dewey 1916:8). A number of other prominent educationalists have also followed the same spirit of Dewey (1916) by advocating the view that schools should aim towards creating and sustaining a 'common culture'. Monocultural schools and, by extension, faith schools, are considered to be the antithesis of the desired objective of common schools. Despite some concerns relating to how 'common values' are defined and who defines these values (Halstead 2008; Haydon 2008), nevertheless common schools within this perspective are seen to provide a sense of equality, equal respect and social justice. More crucially, if the formal education

> ...of young people were to achieve its fundamental purpose of preparing the next generation to live harmoniously together, despite the important differences in culture that the students bring to that community. More positively, the intermingling of those differences in the community of the school would be seen as an enrichment of those very differences.
>
> (Pring 2008:1)

The above approach to integration and schooling is based upon principles associated with the social contact thesis. The social contact thesis is predicated upon established academic research (Hewstone 2006; Wagner et al. 2006; Cantle 2005; Thomas 2011) which has supported the idea that greater contact between different ethnic groups is a useful indicator for reducing levels of prejudice among groups. A number of leading researchers on the contact thesis, including Hewstone (2006), have long argued that it's the *quality* and the *nature* of contact, and not ephemeral contact, which reduces levels of prejudice – it is meaningful contact which plays significant roles in tackling antipathy and enmity among different racial and cultural groups. There is compelling evidence that supports the idea of social contact to reduce prejudice within schools. Academic literature from the United States, which has operated a policy of racial desegregation since the case of Brown v. Board of Education in 1954, has been a focal point for academic research assessing social contact within schools (Wells et al. 2005; Erick 2010).

As already indicated in the previous chapter, social contact theory has been used by a number of local authorities as 'a cornerstone of community cohesion practice' (Cantle 2005:116), especially following the 2001 race riots in some northern English towns. Nevertheless, it is broadly agreed amongst social contact theorists that declining levels of prejudice towards different ethnic groups is not simply based upon contact between different ethnic groups, but is rather predicated on a range of issues, such as the duration of contact, the voluntary or non-voluntary nature of contact and the nature of group perception (Allport 1979; Hewstone and Brown 1986). In fact, social scientists have identified five conditions for effective social contact (Amir 1969; Cook 1978, cited in Short 2002). First, the social space must provide an opportunity for 'real acquaintance'; the people in question 'should get to know each other as individuals' (Short 2002:568). Second, the social space should be free from prejudice or the reinforcement of any stereotypes. Third, contact between groups should be a coming together of groups of equals. Fourth, it 'should be [a] mutually interdependent relationship' (ibid.). Finally, contact should be based upon 'equality and equalitarian inter-group association' (ibid.).

The above policy of school academies to create integrated schools as a way of reducing 'extremism' through cohesion or social contact should be interpreted in the light of the above conditions of social contact. An assessment by Miah (2012) of the approaches to creating integration within the above schools has highlighted how they fall short on a number of key indicators required for meaningful social contact, as highlighted by Short (2002). First, the social political context of the school merger policies is embedded within a climate of fear and antagonism associated with Muslim communities. Some of these antagonisms are motivated by the rise of far-Right organisations such as the English Defence League, Infidels of Britain and Britain First (Goodwin 2011). These organisations have also been actively involved in a number of street protests throughout Britain over several educational issues, such as halal foods, the building of mosques and Muslim faith schools. Second, the political contexts, instead of challenging some of these issues, have fuelled popular concerns over Muslims through racialised security discourses. The nature, intensity and impacts of these policies on Muslim communities were succinctly summarised by the National Association of Muslim Police whilst giving evidence to the House of Commons Select Committee:

> Never before has a community been mapped in a manner and nor it will be...The hatred towards Muslims has grown to a level that defies all logic and is an affront to British values. The climate is such that Muslims are subject to daily abuse in a manner that would be ridiculed by Britain, where [sic] this to occur anywhere else.
>
> (Davies 2010, cited in Husband and Alam 2011:102)

Thirdly, these social policy and political contexts fuel a White backlash, motivate White flight and contribute towards racial conflicts (Miah 2012). For example, the following response to the relocation of Grange schools from a predominantly Bangladeshi community to a mainly White neighbourhood in Royton, Oldham demonstrates how the framing of the school mergers not only undermines but actively works against the common school principles highlighted above.

> Moving students from Grange to a new school on Our Lady's site [Royton] is part of a plan for *'integration via the back door?'* If this goes ahead a time will come when future generations of the ethnic minority families will move to Royton...in time the indigenous population could well move out.
>
> (O.E.C., cited in Miah 2012:34)

The role of history is also important in shedding light on the effectiveness of the above measure as advocated by New Labour policies. In fact, the above policies revive the memory of the 1960s policy of *bussing* which was adopted by 11 local authorities with a significant Black and Minority Ethnic population (BME) (Tomlinson 2008). In fact the policy of bussing was restricted after a group of White parents in the Southall district of London complained to the then Minister of Education, Edward Boyle. They claimed that the 'educational progress of their children was being inhibited in those schools containing large numbers of non-White, mainly South Asian pupils' (Troyna 2003:71). Following Edward Boyle's intervention 'Boyle's Law' was introduced, requiring a 30 per cent cap on BME pupils in a given school, following its support by the Department of Education and Science in 1965 (Troyna 2003).

Given the moral panic around Muslim communities and the problematisation of a range of issues, including halal food, gender segregation and radicalisation, some non-Muslim parents may well want to use parental choice in shaping and maintaining racial separatism (Cumper 1994). Perhaps the most famous historical example of this was captured by the Parental Alliance for Choice in Education (PACE), which supported the predominantly White parents of Thornhill in refusing to send their children to a school in a predominantly Asian area of Savile Town, as required by Kirklees Council, West Yorkshire. Instead, the parents decided to set up a makeshift school above a pub in Thornhill whilst awaiting a judicial review which was held at the High Court in July 1988 (Naylor 1989). On the second day of the judicial review the demands of PACE were accepted, and the important theme arising from this case study is the way in which the campaign and, ultimately, the 'White flight' were framed as tension 'between individual freedom and the public good' and the shortcomings of 'multicultural education'. More recently, researchers in the East End of London have documented how education was instrumental in residential White flight (Dench et al. 2006). They found a number of strategies adopted by White parents to maintain educational segregation; they demonstrated how White parents could get their children to White or Whiter schools within the borough or could move their children to a school outside the borough without changing their residential address. Or they could even uproot and move residential areas so that they are located in an area within a predominantly White catchment area. The East End study, similar to Naylor's (1989), presented White flight not as a radicalised discourse, but as a rational act grounded in White residents' view of the local

Asian community as lowering the standards of education. It also perceived local schools to be neglecting the educational needs of White children by putting greater emphasis on responding to the cultural needs of Asian pupils.

Conclusion

The question of segregation and isolation of Muslim communities, through both Muslim schools and ethnically segregated state schools, is marked by the perception of a problematic presence, especially in light of the 2001 racial disturbances but more poignantly following the events of the London bombings. In many respects the logic of ethnic segregation leading towards racial violence, as documented in the 2001 race riots reports, was extended to argue that segregation along both physical and cultural lines could ultimately lead to extremism and violent extremism. The merging of community cohesion with *soft* counter-terrorism ideas is often defined through the constructs of liberalism as a normative discourse which is ultimately linked to Britishness as an oppositional framing of Islam and Muslim communities. The New Labour school academy policy of creating ethnically mixed schools in some of the 'problematic' Muslim neighbourhoods in England as a de-radicalisation imperative can be seen as definitive test case for examining the public policy framing of Muslim communities through de-radicalisation strategies.

This chapter has provided two concrete examples of integration policies and how they have merged with the objective of maintaining social order in society; the community cohesion and the Prevent approaches to integration are essentially social order discourses, both of these attempting to reduce social unrest or prevent acts of extremism. Mixed schools were seen to facilitate the process of integration, whilst monocultural state schools in general and monocultural Muslim faith schools in particular were seen as hampering the process of integration. Monocultural schools, be they state funded or independent faith schools, and the desired ethnically mixed schools have been the dualistic feature of educational policy as advocated by the government. The former are seen as potentially damaging to the social fabric of society, whilst the latter have been actively pursued by the government in some dominant Muslim neighbourhoods.

It has been argued in this chapter that the emphasis on preventing extremism in general and violent extremism in particular has been the dominant approach in British race relation policies in education within the last decade. This is a significant and a poignant shift away from previous approaches to anti-racism, equal opportunities or multiculturalism by British educational policy. More crucially, the current approach to race, religion and education problematises Muslim pupils within schools as it conflates education with securitisation and counter-terrorism, thus blurring the boundaries between schooling and social control.

Part II

4
Mixed School Imperative and the Question of Self-Segregation

> A key defining feature of the South Asian children by
> teachers...was that 'they do not mix'. This apparent failure
> to mix...was regarded as being as a result of 'their' culture
> and religion and, linked to this, their reluctance to 'inte-
> grate'.
>
> (Crozier and Davies 2008:289)

One of the central themes emerging from the debates on integration and schooling is the idea of Muslim self-segregation. Indeed, both the political and policy rhetoric reinforces the view that Muslim communities want to maintain an idea of separateness by creating both cultural and spatial barriers. A key government policy imperative emerging from the previous chapters is the desire to create ethnically mixed schools in areas with high concentrations of Muslim pupils in order to tackle urban disorder, global terrorism and Muslim fundamentalism (Davies 2008; DCSF 2008).

This chapter will challenge the view of Muslim self-segregation by demonstrating how Muslim pupils view ethnically mixed schools as an ideal type of schooling. The first part considers how mixed schools are characterised by positive experiences which nurture cultural and social capital. It shows how pupils view integration as a form of commodity which can be used as an exchange value during the transition from childhood to adulthood. Whilst the idea of ethnically mixed schools is considered to be the ideal type of schooling, nevertheless there are wider issues which prevent this type of experience being overtly romanticised. It presents the wider political issues and the inability of state policies to challenge anti-Muslim racism as undermining and potentially damaging the 'common school' ideal by 'pushing' pupils to stick together in order to protect themselves against racial harassment.

Most popular and state discourses of integration are one-dimensional in that they view integrated or ethnically mixed schools as positive spaces of hope and segregated schools as recipes for social disorder. This particular worldview is shaped by UK history, especially through the Northern Ireland experience, whereby conflicts between Protestantism and Catholicism are perpetuated through distinctive educational experiences of Catholic and Protestant pupils in separate schools. This template entered the framing of ethnic tensions within the UK through the 2001 race riots and later through the London bombings in July 2005. Despite the questions arising from transporting templates, which is rooted in the particular history, experience and struggles within the Irish and Protestant experience in order to understand Muslims in the UK, there are wider problems associated with constructing mixed schooling through this prism. The key fundamental problem associated with this one-dimensional policy framing is that it fails to recognise how the compounded nature of integration within Muslim discourse is experienced. This chapter demonstrates how positive experiences of mixed schools, which are seen as ideal spaces for nurturing both cultural and social capital, are compounded by fears of anti-Muslim racism that paradoxically replaces segregation between schools with segregation within schools.

Mixed school imperative: 'You know it's all about mixing'

Social contact theory is seen by many as 'a cornerstone of community cohesion practice' (Cantle 2005:116); as a result it has become a highly influential tool within local government thinking. As already noted in the previous chapter, contact hypothesis is based upon the idea that repeated cross-cultural and inter-group contact is a determining factor in understanding the levels of prejudice against different ethnic groups. Whilst there is ample evidence to support the social contact theory (Wagner et al. 2006; Hewstone et al. 2007; Cantle 2008; Thomas 2011), it is broadly agreed amongst contact theorists that declining levels of prejudice towards different ethnic groups are predicated on a range of issues such as duration of contact, voluntary or non-voluntary nature of contact, nature of group perception and size of the ethnic population (Alport 1979; Hewstone and Brown 1986).

The notion of size of population determining the levels of prejudice has been of particular interest amongst researchers; for example, Halstead (1988) shows how a limit of 33 per cent was used by the government to bus Muslim pupils to mainly White schools during the 1960s. More recently, Forman (2003), using evidence from a nationwide sample of Black students in the United States, found that high levels of prejudice were experienced in schools if the Black population rose above 35 per cent (cited in Hewstone 2006:103).

The social contact thesis can also been seen as a meta-narrative in both understanding and challenging the ideas of self-segregation. For Muslims the function of integration is the act of 'mixing' between people of different ethnic backgrounds. Mixing is not seen as one-dimensional with Muslims having sole responsibility for carrying the burden for integration, rather mixing is a reciprocal process. This idea of integration should be 'mutual process of being accepted and accepting' (Sardar 2009:19). Unlike the framing of integration within political and policy discourse, the imperative to mix is a civic duty for all and not a burden for one particular community or group.

An ethnically mixed school provides Muslim pupils with ideal spaces for mixing which provide both individual and collective opportunities. The discourse of mixed school imperative is best understood through the following fundamental themes. First, mixed schooling allows Muslim pupils to get to know one another; it allows students of different ethnic and cultural backgrounds to nurture bonding capital. Second, mixed schools are seen as a microcosm of wider multicultural society; for most pupils, schooling is a key medium through which integration is achieved and actualised. Finally, the discourse of mixing helps shape pupils' understanding of a diverse multicultural society.

Cultural difference and religious identity are essential for all pupils, and is considered to be too important to be confined within the private domain; as a result, mixed schools provide a space for these cultural identities to be debated and negotiated. It is within the context of schooling in general and the classroom environment in particular that a safe space for mixing between people of different cultural backgrounds can be provided.

School spaces are considered to be organic and neutral, and evolving due to students' keen interest in recognising one another's cultural differences (Taylor 1992). These settings should not organised or managed by the school; instead, they should by evolving contexts in which students take a keen interest in getting to know one another. This is demonstrated by the discussion highlighted below, showing how integration is predicated upon mixing or socialising with people. Mixing is seen to occur naturally without teacher involvement or intervention; it occurs voluntarily and spontaneously; more importantly, it is driven by pupils' willingness to know. The idea of mixing was also considered an empowering experience as it provided a platform for cultural exchange and debate. This is clear from the following interaction between students in a mixed comprehensive school in Manchester.

> *What do you mean by mixing?*
> You know just socialising and integrating.
>
> *S. In what context?*
> In school and in class, like in this school and this class there are a lot of mixing we all like to mix and interact. We do this not because teachers tell us, but because we are interested in finding out about different cultures.

The above theme of acknowledging ones cultural identity and the important role that plays in shaping dialogue within public spaces confirms and extends the idea of the 'politics of difference' (Modood 2010). It confirms how religious identity, like other forms of identity, 'should not be privatised and tolerated but should be part of the public space' (Modood 2010:42). The above example, together with observation highlighted below, demonstrates how Muslim pupils view public space as neutral places where aspects of identity and religion can be debated freely.

> I think it's a great idea; you get to know and understand and find out about different people and their backgrounds. Also it helps you to find out what they believe and what they don't believe. They can find out about us about Muslims and what we believe.

Mixing a religious imperative

Muslims are considered to be in a privileged position to mix or to get to know each other, feeling that there is a Quranic imperative for young people to engage in dialogue with students who are ethnically and culturally different. The idea of getting to know each other is taken from the following Quranic verse:

> O mankind! We created you from a single (pair) of a male and a female, and made you into nations and tribes, that ye may know each other (not that ye may despise each other). Verily the most honoured of you in the sight of God is (he who is) the most righteous of you. And God has full knowledge and is well acquainted.
>
> (Quran: 49:13)

The Quranic narrative starts with the premise of cultural difference and diversity, diversity being an essential feature of human creation which is seen as one of the signs of God; the participation of cultural dialogue and exchange is a process of fulfilling the above Quranic worldview. The textual imperative to integrate through getting to know each other has been expanded by a number of academics and theologians. For example, March (2009a, 2009b), drawing upon the works of contemporary traditional scholars such as Mawlawi and others (Sheikh Yusuf al-Qardawi, Sheikh Abd Allah Bin Bayya), argues how one of the conditions for Muslims living in the West is to partake in *dawah*, although *dawah* here is not understood in its conventional sense of proselytising; rather, it incorporates a complex set of terms, drawing from the Quranic narrative, including (1) good-willed exhortation; (2) argumentation; (3) non-coercion and (4) wisdom (March 2009b:76). For Mawlawi, these conditions cannot be fulfilled without social interaction and the forming of bonds, trust and affectionate feelings towards non-Muslims. Indeed, as Mawlawi has pointed out, the idea of *hub al-fitr* (innate love) towards non-Muslims should be nurtured and sustained. This is contrasted with love towards one's fellow Muslims which he argues is based on *hub al-aqidah* (love based on the Muslim creed). Thus, as March (2009b:78) argues, bonds between communities should be based on 'common interest, shared experience and secular virtue', and love for one's fellow Muslim brother does not mean the hatred of fellow non-Muslims. The parallels between the theological articulation of diversity and the lived reality of Muslim pupils within schools are elucidated in the following observation.

> If you walk around the school playground you will find that people of all cultures mix together. As Muslims we accept that all people are different from different religious and races abilities and disabilities. People speak different languages and eat different foods. So as Muslims we have to recognise these differences. In fact, I think there is a verse in the Quran about this. We bring these differences to school; we talk about it in the playground and lunchtime. You know sometimes we agree and other time we don't.

Integration as intercultural dialogue

What is interesting to note is that the imperative to mix happens in the school setting; more importantly, it recognises that students embody a discourse of cultural difference, which can often draw upon religious and non-religious repertoires. Whilst it is common for pupils to provide examples of dialogue between students based on ethnic or religious markers, the following accounts demonstrate how wider issues, including dietary needs and even aspects of sexuality, are also key aspects of discussion and learning. On a wider note, the observation cited below has a number of wider pedagogical implications, based upon the recognition that learning about cultural difference is initiated by the student's desire to learn, which is deeply rooted in everyday schooling experience.

> We learn about many issues by talking to people of different cultural backgrounds. Religion is one issue. But there are many other examples, obviously when you go to the canteen that sparks many conversations about food, you know some people are veggies and other Hindu people won't touch meat... There are also some teachers who are you know... gay. And some kids are also like that. Some people like to make fun, but we chat, sometimes people accept that they are like that and that's what they do, so safe. You know society is like that, people have to recognise that the society is different.

Britain is considered by Muslim pupils as a de facto multicultural society, with mixing being seen as a mechanism through which multiculturalism was actualised. As one of the respondents remarked: 'it's part of multicultural Britain isn't it. How are you going to be multicultural if you do not mix?' The process of mixing occurred because pupils had a genuine desire to find out about cultural differences among their cohorts. Mixing was seen as an active process shaped by a multicultural template of integration, which provided an opportunity for pupils to participate in civic multiculturalism. Pupil discourses recognised the importance of cultural difference, which included not only ethnic differences but also perspectives on subcultural diversity. These discourses recognised the need to respect both individual autonomy and group differences and, in doing so, also recognised that human beings are diverse and culturally embedded, that cultural diversity is inescapable and desirable and, most importantly, the importance given to intercultural dialogue (Parekh 2000).

Intercultural dialogue or interculturalism has recently entered the social policy lexicon (Cantle 2012). Interculturalism essentially puts more emphasis on dialogue and an even greater emphasis on individual rights as opposed to group rights. For some, the idea of interculturalism complements the process of multiculturalism (Meer and Modood 2012), whilst others feel that interculturalism will replace multiculturalism as a conceptual policy framework (Cantle 2012). For Muslim discourse, intercultural dialogue is a hallmark of multiculturalism. Mixing within the intercultural context is achieved within a discursive framework; it is only through the act of speech and exchange of cultural references that the objectives of mixing are achieved. It is through the act of discourse that young people construct their experiences, challenge their own prejudices and, above all, construct their own versions of social reality. The importance of dialogue in the act of integration is best exemplified by the following by a Muslim pupil.

> You have to talk to people to get to know them, otherwise you end up making things up; you have to integrate before you can get to know each other.

A mixed school provides a space for students of different cultural and religious backgrounds to get to know each other. Mixed schools within pupil discourse are characterised by social spaces not dominated by any one ethnic group, but rather as spaces comprising a range of ethnic groups. The following responses taken from two separate focus groups best exemplify this point. The first example is taken from a focus group in Oldham; it shows how meaningful and detailed interaction between Muslims and non-Muslims can lead towards greater trust and stronger bonds. It further recognises how social contact could help reduce racial prejudice between the Muslim community and the wider public. The idea of combating antagonism and animosity through greater social contact did not come as a surprise, especially given the history of racial conflict and tension in some of the areas where the focus groups took place. The second observation is from south Manchester, and shows how mixed schools best equip students for the future. Both examples provide an insight into how mixed schools are framed. Moreover, they show how schools are perceived as active spaces in which pupils can understand cultural differences.

> You see if you go to a mixed school you get to see other people and you get to know other people … It helps break down prejudice [from both sides] and helps people build trust.

and

> I think it's a great idea; you get to know and understand about different people and their cultural backgrounds. The real world is made up of people of different backgrounds and this helps you to prepare for that I agree with that you get to know and find out about people of different backgrounds.

'This is a mixed school … '

This section examines how students understand their own [mixed] schools by comparing them to neighbouring segregated schools in the same borough. One of the many ways pupils do this is through a racialised binary discourse: schools with a significant White or Asian cohort are viewed as 'all-White' or 'all-Asian schools'. Schools with a mainly diverse cohort without one dominant ethnic group are characterised as mixed schools – this is a significant point to note, especially given how the educational discourses cited in Chapter 2 highlighted how mixed schools are characterised as spaces with a dominant White cohort and minority ethnic intake.

The racial dynamics of schools within each borough were found to be central to young pupils; from an early age they developed a detailed knowledge of all the borough's segregated or mixed schools. They were able to provide concrete examples of most schools in their borough that were racially segregated. It appeared that there was a consensus on segregated and mixed schools; moreover, there was an acknowledgement by Muslim students that mixed schools provided a more complete and well-rounded education than the segregated ones. Mixed schools were suitable not because of the educational standards they offered but because of the quality of experience they provided. The following observation by a Muslim female student from a school in the East End of London highlights how attending a mixed school with a range of diverse communities helps reduce levels of prejudice; it further notes how the mixed school experience allows individuals to be 'better and more tolerant' people. This way of framing mixed schools within the context of social contact theory further supports wider academic studies on the contact hypothesis discussed in previous chapters (Alport 1979; Short 2002), which states that regular inter-group contact provides appropriate conditions for reducing prejudice.

> *S. How would you describe this school?*
> I think this will be a mixed school … a very very mixed. You have many people from different cultural backgrounds Black, Asians, English and Europeans and yeah mixed race. It's a good idea for people of different religion and culture to learn together. I think it makes people better. What do you mean 'makes people better'? You know, better person, more tolerant person.

Ethnic school segregation was an important feature for most Muslim students, and it did not come as a surprise that all focus group respondents were able to provide concrete examples of segregated schools. Within each respective borough, this clearly shows how the type and nature of the school informs the way in which education and schooling is debated. It is worth pointing out that the schools they described as segregated were not schools that had been widely debated in the public domain. It seems that the pupils were reversing the popular discourse of segregated 'Muslim' schools with mono-cultural [White] schools. The example cited below demonstrates how schools are defined in racial terms. In the following case, Muslim pupils chose to describe monocultural White schools as segregated; this is contrary to the way segregated schools are framed by the national media. The schools that tend to receive much of the attention in Oldham are those in which Muslims account for over 90 per cent of the students. The above observation provides a good example of the way in which the popular public discourse of segregation is reversed. This is clear from the following example:

> *S. Can you give me any examples of schools which are segregated?*
> Mountthill, Railsworth. You see most of these schools don't get mentioned in the media, most of the time they are only interested in pointing out Asian or Muslim schools. Nobody talks about the white schools.

As noted in the above observation, schools that generated a significant amount of public and policy attention because of their monocultural composition did not feature in the immediate discourse. Rather, White schools located in predominantly White neighbourhoods were cited. This further shows how the pupil discourse rejects the public debate on segregation as simply focusing on state Muslim schools. It is worth noting that the choice of expression used to describe the educational experience did not reflect the language of 'cohesion' – in other words, no references were made to schools which were 'integrated' or 'cohesive' as reflected within the public discourse of Oldham. Instead they had their own language to describe the nature of the schools. Mixed compulsory educational institutions were described in either visual or numerical terms, and most focus group respondents had a clear picture of the diverse range encompassing their own school and surrounding schools. Mixed schools were viewed as an ideal educational setting by most Muslim pupils; this was because they were able to provide students with the relevant and necessary skills required for a rounded education. This point is further articulated by a young girl from Oldham:

> It's better if you come to a mixed school because there are many benefits. There are narrow-minded people I'm not saying this

because they are white. I'm saying this because Asians can be narrow-minded. You can think people are so strange because they are from different cultural backgrounds. If they didn't attend a mixed school they would not have had that opportunity to find out that they are OK. There are good and bad people in all cultures.

Doing integration: integration as performance

The above observations clearly demonstrate a strong narrative of Muslims mixing with people of different cultural backgrounds, in doing so this challenges some of the commentaries associated with 'Muslim ghettos', 'parallel lives' or the idea of self-segregation. It further demonstrates the importance placed by Muslim pupils on intercultural dialogue based upon socio-economic perspectives but also drawn from religious repertoires. Whilst the above examples focused upon the act of integration, evidence highlighted below stresses the need for Muslims to be *seen* to be integrating.

This idea of integration as performance, in light of the public debate on Muslim and integration in the UK and also in many European countries, was central to the discursive function. The focus group interviews cited below confirm that young Muslims 'do' mix with non-Muslims; this can be observed in schools and also within wider society. They also demonstrate the need for public recognition and, above all, acceptance of Muslim integration in the same way that other communities, such as African Caribbean communities, have been recognised. This is one of the reasons why many of the interviewees used the example of British boxing champion Amir Khan to argue their case. The choice of Amir Khan is not surprising, especially given the prominent role that sport in general – and boxing in particular – plays in debating racial identity; after all, Frank Bruno and Chris Eubank during the early 1990s were promoted within popular culture as iconic figures of Black Britishness. In similar ways, both New Labour and the media promoted Amir Khan as a positive role model for multi-ethnic Britain during the crucial period of the 2004 Olympic Games and the London bombings in 2005 (Burdsey 2007).

Muslims do integrate . . . [For example,] in school and also, in town, you see shop with different Asian people working or generally mixing. You also see in your own community, there are people of different backgrounds and you just get on with your neighbours it's one of those things. It's like Amir Khan, he uses the flag and says he's British Muslim and he is fighting for Britain. We are integrating more so than other communities. You see Muslim community is a new community and within short amount of time I think we have come a long way compared to say the Jewish or other communities.

The example cited below continues the same vein of argument based upon the crucial idea of integration as performance, by drawing upon changing cultural patterns of dietary habits amongst young Muslims. It provides a sociological observation of the growth in mainstream fast-food outlets in responding to the rising demand of the purchasing power of Muslim youth. As a result, a number of high street food chains have now begun to offer halal food – for example, the Trafford Centre in Trafford, Greater Manchester, is a case in point; a significant number of restaurants and fast-food outlets situated within the food aisles cater for Muslim shoppers, and it also has dedicated space for people of all faith backgrounds to make use of its quiet room for prayers. One of the main explanations for this cultural shift is based on the desire for Muslims to be seen as part of the mainstream, but also to be able to share the same public space with other communities. More importantly, it is argued that this symbolic shift in culture confirms the idea of integration as a conscious act, which can be used to silence some of the critics of Islam who argue that Muslim communities are inward looking and do not want to mix with people of other cultural or ethnic backgrounds.

> In Manchester there are so many restaurants that serve halal food. What I find interesting is when KFC started to go halal [in some towns] all Muslim flocked there. The question is why? When you have all other chicken places run by Muslims, why do Muslim still go to KFC... It's because Muslims want to seen to be integrating. I am sure people do this to show Muslim haters... look we do integrate!

Interrupting and rupturing the mixed school imperative
The previous section highlighted the variety of ways in which mixing was seen and was considered to be both a social and a religious imperative. Ethnic integration for Muslims is considered to be a valuable

medium through which social and cultural capital in a multicultural society is achieved; it also facilitates different ways in which Muslims view citizenship and participation in a multicultural society.

This section will demonstrate how mixing does not constitute a normative experience for Muslim pupils, and in many respects it appears to be a counter-narrative to the imperative for mixing. It is worth pointing out that superficially it may appear to be a contradictory response to mixing, but in reality the idea of 'sticking together' is far more complex. First, it recognises the fact that loyalty to an in-group does not translate into disloyalty to an out-group. This point was strongly argued in the previous section by drawing upon the theological writings of Mawlawi and others (March 2009a). Second, whilst intercultural dialogue, mixing and getting to know each other is a key feature for Muslims in ethnically mixed schools, these moments of positive dialogue can be interrupted at times or even ruptured due to external factors. Third, experiences and perceptions of racism, combined with the deeply politicised context of Islam within contemporary society, can contribute to a sense of solidarity, ethnic clustering and overall sense of ambivalence within mixed schools. Pupil narratives presented in this section reinforce wider empirical evidence that supports the idea that racism and the global War on Terror are shaping Muslim school experiences (Crozier and Davies 2008).

Racism and Schooling: 'At the end of the day you're still a Paki'

The discourse of sticking together or ethnic clustering is reinforced by experiences of racism and anti-Muslim prejudice within the school environment, which consists of both direct and overt forms of racism by fellow pupils and also more subtle covert forms of institutionalised racism. International events and the rhetoric of the War on Terror have also nurtured a sense of hostility displayed by non-Muslim pupils and teaching staff towards Muslim pupils. The accounts of anti-Muslim prejudice within schools often coincides with the emergence and popular appeal of 'new British fascism' (Goodwin 2011) in the form of the far-Right street protest group, the English Defence League (EDL). The politics of the EDL, with its ability to construct violent forms of masculinity aimed at the Muslim 'other', is often played out within school premises. The anger, resentment and disenchantment arising from the War on Terror or other forms of social inequality can often lead to direct confrontations within schools. Some of the far-Right influences amongst pupils generated by direct action and massive street mobilisations in many towns and cities in the UK have given some White young men a 'heroic' voice. Some of the far-Right causes have directly impacted upon schooling, especially the campaign against halal foods on school menus fuelled by EDL. These 'concerns' against the alleged socio-political threat generated by Muslims post-9/11 and -7/7 are further galvanised by pupils to create animosity within schools. Some of these experiences have played a vital role in reinforcing Muslim group solidarity based primarily on religion, thus acting as a support mechanism in the absence of any institutional support mechanism. In order to support these observations, concrete examples of hostility towards Muslims in the UK and also within school premises can be cited. The following examples, taken from an ethnically mixed school in the north-west of England, provide supporting evidence of anti-Muslim prejudice influenced by the rise of the EDL. The examples cited below are particularly revealing as they demonstrates concrete examples of the ways in which far-Right activity outside school premises has created hostility and feelings of isolation within schools. They further demonstrate how accounts of racism and anti-Muslim prejudice are internalised and actualised by members of staff, and how in return this influences the experience of schooling. Observations of racism show how the question of safety is paramount for Muslim parents and pupils, especially in light of the evidence 'that racist abuse is a lived experience for some on a daily basis, but for all as a feature of their schooling' (Crozier and Davies 2008:295).

Sometimes it gets really tensed in schools especially after the EDL demos. Whenever there has been an EDL march the White kids come in school and chant 'EE EDL'. Sometimes the chants get very load in the playground or in the canteens. Sometimes we would get really angry and we might shout out 'MM MDL' or Muslim Defence League. We now that no such organisations exist but we have to make our stand... What's the point reporting this? Sometimes the teachers are present when this happens and the do Jack all. You see we are not daft, we know that some teachers have sympathy for some of the stuff the EDL say. I'll give you an example. Some teachers now nothing about Islam, they think that Halal meat is barbaric or some even think that Muslims are medieval or even barbaric. So you tell me? You would be daft to report these to the teachers.

Islam and the War on Terror

Muslim discourses within schools also drew upon wider international experiences of socio-political events. These events not only help shape the way in which pupils view themselves but also the way in which others view them. Focus group accounts demonstrate a strong sense of politicisation of Muslim communities in general and Muslim young people in particular. It is clear that Muslim youths take an active role in following both domestic and international affairs affecting the Muslim community. It is also apparent that 'grievance politics' following the Bush Years (Imtiaz 2010) played a crucial role in developing a sense of collective Muslim identity which helps shape and nurture a sense of Muslim ummah.

The politicisation of young Muslims is demonstrated by the keen interest they show in the headline news reports regarding Muslims in Europe or throughout the 'Muslim' world. The meta-discourse of Muslim pupils usually takes an oppositional reading (Hall 1973) of dominant public discourse on Muslims and Islam. It is important to note that this particular way of reading media events was a universal trait within all the focus groups. In order to form their understanding of 'Muslim events', they often consulted a wide range of media sources ranging from traditional to new media outlets. It is also clear that major political events within the Muslim world formed part of collective conversation in everyday life (Imtiaz 2010; Philips and Iqbal 2010).

International events effecting Muslims in Switzerland, France or even in the United States help create social bonding at a local level. The following account demonstrates how Muslims see themselves as a collective ummah; this theme of collective group spirit, together with external events shaping internal discourse, is continued with the French debate on the veil as cited below. The girls' focus groups showed an active interest in the debate on Islamic dress and secular public space. The politicisation of the hijab in some European countries helped inform and define the general discourse on integration, Muslim identity and anti-Muslim prejudice. Muslim girls felt a strong affinity and solidarity with Muslim women in France; this is further exemplified by the fact that issues of loyalty, acceptance and inclusion were all mediated through the prism of the hijab controversy. The issue of the hijab was one of the key issues discussed by the girls' focus groups. There was no connection between the type of discourse and students wearing the veil; most often, girls who did not wear the hijab projected strong feelings of solidarity with fellow 'Muslim sisters'. The intensity of the feeling expressed below demonstrates how the hijab is worn by Muslim girls as a matter of choice; the statement also demonstrates how Muslims view the double standards associated with choices made by Muslim women and those exercised by non-Muslim women.

> I don't think they mention it as blunt as that, I guess it is more subtle and you get hints now and again that Muslim should integrate and be more western... Did you hear about the French president, he is trying to ban the veil? He was saying like can't remember how he said it but he was trying to say that wearing the hijab is not part of French culture and stuff like that, and if you are a Muslim in France, you can't wear the hijab in school. I think it's very wrong for him to do that and also to say that. It's wrong. It's like, it's stupid! When non-Muslim go out wearing no clothes its fine because its women making a choice. But as soon Muslims want to wear the hijab it's such an abomination... Its strange and it makes me very angry.

International events play a crucial role in defining and framing integration; Muslim pupils display particular interest in political events involving fellow Muslims throughout the world. An example which helps elucidate this point further involves the case of the Gaza bombing in 2008. Some of the interviews were conducted whilst the siege of Gaza was being played out in the media, and thus it came as no surprise to find that young Muslims paid particular attention to the details of the bombings. It was particularly interesting that a group of year 7 (aged 12) boys drew links between the siege of Gaza and the global war against Islam. As noted below, young people were able to draw upon a range of tools to criticise the *received knowledge* of key political events through mainstream media. The young people recognised how the media position themselves as diametrically opposed to the issues and concerns facing the Muslim community. The institutional racist usage of front page headlines as a way of conveying particular readings of events was seen as a means of promoting messages to reflect the problematic nature of Muslim communities, and is further exemplified by the following observation.

I think you have to stick together with your own because there is a war. Yeah you only have to look at Gaza some people make a big deal about Muslims because of 9/11. You know if something happens with Muslims like terrorist bomb or something like that it's always in the front page but you know if it's a Muslim that gets killed no one cares that much but like if a English person gets killed they make a big thing and they even make a big ceremony. But if a Muslim person that is killed by a terrorist bomb or killed they call him a terrorist.

The connection between 'Muslims as terrorists' within the news media and similar depictions of Muslims in the wider media helps shape young Muslim attitudes towards the mainstream media and, in return, influences the how Muslims perceive the question of integration. The question for Muslims is related less to issues of self-segregation than to those concerning the acceptance and treatment of Muslims within public discourse with dignity and self-respect. In light of this, young people develop a critical reading of the 'Muslim folk devil' as portrayed in the media (Alexander 2000). It is clear that such pathological impressions of Muslims inform the self-definition of Muslim communities, and it is also important to note that the perceptions of Muslims emanating from the media can have a crucial impact on feelings of isolation and alienation. This is clear from the following observation, made by a 12-year-old boy in Manchester, which captures the feelings generated by the negative media depiction of Muslims as terrorists.

It makes me feel not important or accepted it just makes me feel that I'm alone in a world of darkness.

Sticking together: Constructing 'ummahtic' space in schools

Muslim students in mixed schools talked of developing a range of complex and creative ways of responding to dominant hegemonic Whiteness (Gilborn 2008) by defining and redefining the rules of engagement. Whiteness is a social construct which is linked to ideology and the social status of people socially and culturally identified as White. Whiteness is understood to be a central signifier, deeply rooted within history, representing power and authority of certain people over others in society. Hegemonic Whiteness sees schools as possible hostile spaces for Muslim students, spaces which were defined, first, by the numerical dominance of White students in a given school. Second, there is an understanding that the existence of a school where White pupils are in the majority could lead to the racial privileging of White students over non-Whites. Third, these notions of hostility are often predicated upon personal experiences of racism and anti-Muslim prejudice, based upon the personal (e.g. hostility towards the hijab) together with the institutional (e.g. policies, school ethos) responses to cultural differences. Finally, the role played by international events, such as the War on Terror, should be used to understand the changing dynamics of schooling for Muslim pupils.

Ethnic clustering within the context of schools is thus seen as a way of responding to hegemonic Whiteness within schools, and also the hostility arising from the War on Terror. One of the main strategies discussed by Muslim pupils to challenge hegemonic Whiteness in schools was the idea of sticking together: sticking together functions when a group of students of similar religion consciously cluster together, as a way of generating support and strength, in the face of a perceived or actual hostile school environment. An important theme emerging from the discourse of sticking together is that it transcends markers of ethnic difference and unites young people on the basis of shared experiences. For example, statements such as 'we Muslims all need to stick together' or 'we have to look out for each other' provide young people with a way of achieving 'safety in numbers'. Perhaps the most important features of sticking together is that it 'just happens'; it is akin to a subconsciously conditioned response to perceived hostile environments. Ethnic clustering is not rule-governed;

rather, it is an organic process in which people of a particular faith or ethnic background wilfully navigate towards one another, based upon shared experiences and concerns. There is no malicious intent behind the idea of sticking together; in fact, as indicated in the previous chapter, pupils often socialise and 'mix' with people of different ethnic and religious backgrounds. This point was made with great passion by one focus group member in a mainly mixed school in Oldham.

> It's not like oh she's Muslim and I'm going to hang around with them, it just happens that we are both Muslims. If there was a new kid in class and they were English, white or whatever, it won't be that I don't want to hang about with them. What happens is if there are problems outside the school it can have an impact on how we are treated. So you know we have to stick together. Most of the times people can tell the difference between a Sikh, Hindu or a Muslim, so you will find that all Asians will stick together – that what you have to do!

Sticking together is not considered as a negative force responsible for undermining individuality and self-reliance. Rather, it is seen as a positive act which helps students against a number of issues, including racism, bullying and anti-social behaviours such as drug taking and alcohol abuse. More importantly, sticking together nurtures a social support mechanism beyond the traditional or secular institutional infrastructures such as family, teachers and youth workers.

Sticking together reaches its peak during certain times of the school day; these times are usually personalised times, such as during break and lunchtimes. If the schools are located in a predominantly White neighbourhood then sticking together may be exemplified by the perceived essential practice among up to a dozen pupils, travelling to and from the school. One of the many reasons for this is based on the way in which Muslim pupils perceive certain geographical spaces as hostile; these may be neighbourhoods with large concentrations of White people or schools located in mainly White residential areas with a history of far-Right activities. There are also particular spaces within the school that have the potential to be 'marked' by ethnic clustering and racialised spaces. There were certain areas within the canteen or the playground where Muslim pupils will play, and there are other places where White kids will 'hang about'. These spaces were seen not as territories or fixed spaces that erupted in tension or violence but as spaces that had developed organically over the duration of schooling, and which tended to be determined by sports activities or other related pastimes and hobbies. In fact in one extreme case, Muslim and non-Muslim pupils would choose different times to go to the canteen for their lunch.

Teachers often perceive group solidarity as intimidating or running counter to spirit of community cohesion. As a result, many teachers routinely attempt to break down racialised forms of 'ethnic clustering' through mixed seating, group work and various sports activities, only to find that, in the absence of such factors, sticking together continues as a normalising presence.

There are three main approaches adopted by teachers to challenge the act of sticking together: first, implementation of a standard policy within the class, mixing pupils up; this would be done either by a policy of 'boy-girl, boy-girl' or through alphabetical ordering of names on the register. The second approach would involve a teacher identifying instances of ethnic clustering and directly intervening. Finally, in most cases it was felt that an overtly racialised tone was present in tackling ethnic clustering – teacher interventions challenging the idea of sticking together were routinely administered against Muslim pupils but not White students – thus further reinforcing the view that it is the Muslims that have an issue with integration. In these circumstances it is important to note that pupils did not challenge the teacher's involvement in trying to mix the pupils. This is demonstrated by two examples cited below. The first is taken from a sports lesson at one school and the second during a field trip at another school.

It's like in PE when the teacher will shout at us because there are two trampolines and all the Asian girls will go on one and all the White girls will go on the other. When this happens and it usually does happen the teacher will say 'come on girls. Why don't you mix together?'

We went on a trip once and we just happen to go with our mates and the white lads would also go wither their mates. But the teacher came to us and told us to 'go and mix with them'. Why didn't he go up to the white lads and tell them to come and mix with us... The teachers always think that it's our problem for not mixing.

Conclusion

This chapter problematised the idea of integration as a binary construct. It also challenged the premise that Muslim pupils cluster together for the purpose of maintaining self-segregated communities. Instead it provided accounts by Muslim students in ethnically mixed schools demonstrating how the discourse of integration and schooling can often be seen as complex, ambiguous and contradictory. First, mixed schools were presented as positive spaces based upon the idea of geographical spaces of hope (Philips 2010), and which provided an opportunity for Muslim pupils both to interact and 'do multiculturalism'. This experience, or 'performing integration', was examined through the Quranic lens of 'getting to know each other', which provided data in support of the community cohesion thesis (Cantle 2008) based upon the principles of social contact (Hewstone 2006a) and cultural pluralism. For Muslim pupils, the function of a multicultural template of integration was based upon the act of mixing between people of diverse ethnic and religious backgrounds. Mixing voluntarily occurred within the school environment driven by the desire to know and to understand. Moreover, the idea of mixing was considered as an empowering experience as it provided a platform for cultural exchange and debate in a de facto multicultural society. Most importantly, mixing was actualised within a discursive framework; it was only through the act of speech and exchange of cultural references that the objectives of mixing were achieved. It is through the function of discourse that Muslim pupils constructed their experiences, challenged their own prejudices and, above all, shaped their own versions of social reality.

Second, pupil discourse highlighted how the geographical spaces of hope (Philips 2010) can also produce ambivalent experiences (Bauman 1991), which can reinforce the importance of group solidarity and belonging to a collective body of Muslims. The collective group was constructed through the religious categorisation of group solidarity, which was largely a response to experiences of racism and anti-Muslim prejudice, combined with the depiction of Muslims within the public domain as having a problematic presence. Data in this section demonstrated how experiences of anti-Muslim prejudice within the context of global War on Terror (Imtiaz 2010) played a significant role in shaping Muslim school experiences. These experiences, shaped through pupil and teacher interaction, played a crucial role in politicising young Muslims while at the same time reinforcing group solidarity (Ibn Khaldun 1967) through the process of sticking together. Sticking together occurs when Muslim students consciously cluster together, as a way of generating support and achieving safety in numbers, in the face of a perceived or actual hostile school environment. Muslim pupils did not demonstrate any confidence within the various institutional support mechanisms: instead, it was clear that the discussion of segregation is more a reflection of social exclusion, which is largely brought about through institutional racism and prejudice (Crozier and Davies 2008), rather than any conscious attempt at self-segregation.

5
Intersectionalities and the Question of Self-Segregation

> Some districts are on their way of becoming fully fledged ghettoes – black holes into which no-one goes without fear and trepidation, and from which no-one ever escapes undamaged. The walls are going up around many of our communities, and the bridges...are crumbling. But the aftermath of 7/7 forces us to assess where we are; we are sleep walking our way to segregation. We are becoming strangers to each other, and we are leaving communities to be marooned outside the mainstream.

The above dystopian view of race relations was provided by Trevor Philips (2005) in his role as the chair of the Commission for Racial Equality, a non-governmental public body established to promote race equality and address racial discrimination. The speech, made two months after the London bombings in September 2005, made national and even international headlines and was to have significant impact on the ways in which the question of segregation and Muslim communities were viewed. The political rhetoric surrounding segregation, Muslim pupils and schooling appeared at a time when policy analysts were discussing important two studies conducted by Bristol University. The studies warned of the pervasive nature of ethnic segregation in some UK schools. The first report, published in 2004, demonstrated how residential segregation as one of the principal causes of 'substantial segregation on ethnic criteria in some schools' (Burgess and Wilson 2004:237). More significantly their second report, published in 2006, showed significant levels of ethnic segregation within primary and secondary schools but also ominously suggested that 'school segregation is very substantially (and significantly) greater than is the case with residential segregation' (Johnston et al. 2006:988). Fear and concerns over 'Muslim ghettoes' continued with the publication of the 2011 Census, with fear and concerns over how some towns and cities, including Slough, Luton and London in the UK, have become minority White (Simpson 2012). Further moral panic over population growth and ethnic segregation followed the publication of a well-publicised report by the Policy Exchange which demonstrated how Britain's Black and minority communities could potentially double from 14 to 20–30 per cent by the middle of the century (Sunak and Rajeswaran 2014).

The advocates of self-segregation thesis have often maintained the idea that Muslim communities develop conscious racial boundaries with a willingness to create their own ghettos (Philips 2005; Cary 2008; Nazir-Ali 2008; Ali 2010) in order to preserve fixed and unchanging accounts of cultural and religious practice. Chapter 3 has shown how this construct has led some local authorities in Britain to actively pursue the path of desegregation of some ethnically monocultural schools in the hope of promoting integration and greater social contact between people of different ethnic communities. This chapter will examine wider issues relating to self-segregation, particularly in relation to the following questions: To what extent is this claim of self-segregation based upon lived realities of Muslim communities? Do Muslim communities inadvertently pursue the course of 'voluntary separatism' (Merry 2013)? Can the claim of 'sleepwalking to segregation' Muslim style ever be justified? More crucially, will greater parental choice for Muslim parents further undermine the political debate on the 'shared values' and 'shared futures' of Britain?

Based upon empirical data, this chapter will put forward the argument that the idea of segregation is more predicated upon family circumstances rather that out of choice; in other words, 'those that can send their children to ethnically mixed school, do'. By exploring Muslim attitudes relating to the broader aspects of segregation and schooling, especially within the context of self-segregation, it argues that Muslims, similar to previous migrant communities, feel the need to erect neither a 'community within a community' nor a 'nation within a nation' through formal or informal structures which guarantee the preservation of a normative essence of 'Muslimness'. Rather, similar to the experiences of Muslim girls in Muslim faith schools, Muslim identity is seen as something fluid. In fact, 'Muslimness' within the context of schooling is a complex phenomenon, one that is mediated through a complex set of variables, including race, religion and social class. In short, Muslim consciousness is transformed and shaped through there changing realities and circumstances.

Residential integration: the opening of possibilities

Integration for Muslim communities is a 'lived experience'; in fact the process started with the arrival of the first group of economic migrants to Britain in search of employment and a better life, and has continued through following generations. In many ways for British post-colonial subjects, integration is a natural process and an idea that Muslim communities fully understand, and is considered to be 'in the blood of all migrant groups'. Integration is not a problematic phenomenon; after all, the first generation of migrant communities had already factored this idea in mind when they made the choice to migrate to European soil. More significantly, the shifting of geographical spaces does not undermine notions of religiosity or Muslimness, but rather the Islamic theological imagination provides allowances for change (Abdullah 2004; Ramadan 2010). This understanding that migrant communities have to go through both economic and social transformations broadly reflects the pioneering work on urban sociology conducted by the US-based Chicago School of Sociology (CSS). The CSS, established during the turn of the twentieth century, dedicated its energies to exploring questions of integration and assimilation by combining detained ethnographic fieldwork with social theory at a time when Chicago was undergoing significant changes, with a large influx of migration from Europe. As a result, CSS developed a hypothesis which stated that migrant communities initially settled in the poorest neighbourhoods and gradually, having established financial capital, dispersed into the surrounding suburbs with eventual assimilation into host societies (Park and Burgess 1969). Whilst the question of assimilation is ruled out for Muslims as it was for other minority communities, nevertheless the idea that integration is process governed is fundamental to the Muslim experience.

One of the key principles of integration is residential integration, which allows the opening up of a number of possibilities associated with other forms of integration, such as integrated schools. The links between neighbourhood and school segregation are often contested, for some ethnic school segregation is far greater than ethnic neighbourhood segregation (Johnson et al. 2006). Nevertheless, for Muslim parents residential integration was seen as a stepping stone towards achieving school integration; this is clearly articulated below. Whilst the desire for residential and educational integration exists for most Muslims, as will be made apparent in Chapter 6, the reality is that it can only be achieved by those possessing economic, cultural and social capital (Bourdieu 1986). In light of the close relationship between residential segregation and school segregation, some Muslim communities with the required economical capital are able to speed up the process of integration by gradually moving out of traditional Black and Minority Ethnic (BME) areas. The idea of ethnic clustering within residential neighbourhoods was never meant to be an end in itself – rather a temporary process linked with early patterns of migration and settlement which allowed Muslim communities to achieve confidence, security and maturity before they were able to engage with mainstream society. In many respects the shifting geographical pattern is part of an ongoing process dislocation and relocation experienced by migrant communities. This process of gradual residential integration from segregated neighbourhoods to mixed neighbourhoods, in other words, dispersal of Muslim communities from areas where they had settled, is supported by census data and confirmed by parental observations, cited below. For example, BME communities were living in more mixed areas in 2011 than they did in 2001 and, more crucially, Muslim communities are now less concentrated and more evenly spread then they were in 2001 (Simpson 2012). Conversely, the White population, on average, live in districts with 85 per cent of White British residents whilst all BME communities, on average, live in districts representing 10 per cent of residents (ibid.).

> I'll give you an example: my parents and I have been living in Glodwick since the 1970s. In 2005, in other words after 30 years or so later, I decided to move out into Saddleworth; it is a predominantly white area, so I have already made the leap and so others have also made that leap and made that transition. Living

in Glodwick was always a temporary option. I put my energy into developing a business; once that paid off I was able to more out of Glodwick which is mainly a 'Pakistani area'.

Whilst the above change signifying the preference to moving into racially mixed neighbourhoods, highlighted by the respondent, seems like a small step for the 'outside' community, for the local Muslim community this is a reflection upon an ongoing process whereby migrant communities adapt and readapt to changing circumstances which best serve the process of social mobility. The adjustment from traditional to non-traditional areas represents a major transition and also different ways of doing things, especially given that Muslim neighbourhoods are close-knit entities with strong levels of bonding capital which provide families and individuals with good support structures. This is clearly articulated by the following example. It demonstrates how a transition to non-traditional residential areas is seen as breaking or separating ties with one's group. This particular style of narrative is described in terms of 'sacrifices' that are made by family members who have made the conscious choice to move into mainly White residential areas. Integration in this respect is viewed as a natural progression from the 'early sacrifices that were made by the first generation of Muslims', who took considerable steps in uprooting their own families from Pakistan and Bangladesh to the UK.

I think instances like this go unnoticed by the wider society people tend to focus on the big community and not the little pockets of people that are now moving. I think people who think about integration don't think of the dynamics within our own communities. They don't realise the sacrifices we make, in fact we make far bigger sacrifices than the white communities. Because we are so attached to the communities that we live in and we have to look at the cultures within cultures. Sometimes that I think it is unfair because of the so-called police makers and the decision-makers do not realise these sacrifices that we are making. To them it's the Muslims who are not integrating.

Genuine attempts to integrate into the host society are considered to be in line with the 'migrant ethic', or a form of 'concerted cultivation' (Lareau 2003) whereby parents invest in both the socio-economical and cultural experiences of their children, with the view that it is reciprocated through cultural reproduction. The migrant ethic' underpinned by hard labour, systematic use of time and firm belief in socio-economic progress is largely associated with the notion of social progression and embourgeoisement (Goldthorpe et al. 1963). This migrant ethic can be linked with 'new affluent workers', which was highlighted in the Great British Class Survey, as a social class position with moderate income, small savings and relatively high house values but nevertheless with emerging forms of cultural capital (Savage et al. 2013). The embourgeoisement thesis posits manual workers and their families gradually moving into middle-class neighbourhoods and starting to adopt bourgeois values (Goldthorpe et al. 1963). Muslim experiences of residential integration, especially on the changes arising from the move from traditional monocultural neighbourhoods to prosperous mixed neighbourhoods, correspond with a change in the value system, which signifies a transition from 'communal sociability' towards a more 'privatised form of social existence' (Goldthorpe et al. 1963:76).

The shift from traditional BME to ethnically mixed neighbourhoods opens up a number of possibilities for Muslim communities, such as providing their children with a number of socio-economic opportunities to succeed in life because the choice of residential area is fundamentally connected with better locations or catchment areas for high-achieving schools. Thus, integration is associated with the notion of embourgeoisement and the aspirations of middle-class styles and standards, which are grounded in the premise that integration demonstrates a symbolic change in the prospects and life chances of the immediate family and also the future of their children. Integration within the context of social class is a privilege predicated upon social (Putnam 2000) and cultural capital (Bourdieu and Passerson 1999) and is largely associated with community members who have the financial capacity to move. Those who have had the privilege or the financial means of moving from traditional Muslim residential areas have been seen by others as having 'made it' or having become successful in life – this acknowledgment and recognition by fellow Muslims demonstrates how desegregation is seen not as a problematic symbol but rather as affirmation and confirmation of a social process. This is very clear from the following account of the 'migrant work ethic'.

You see our fathers came here not to cut grass but to make a better future for ourselves and our children. This is a teaching that is in our blood that is why it's important to work hard so that you buy a big house near a good school. You see it is important to invest in yourself and your families. Good house, neighbourhood and expensive cars are all important. You will be respected both by people in this country and also people in Bangladesh. What is the point in working so hard and living in the dumps it makes no sense. Our fathers and uncles worked hard it's our time to ensure that we go on to make a difference to our lives but also to this country. You see it's all about change for the better!

It is clear that 'movement away' from Muslim populations is a given reality, and for some parents it seems that the choices or preferences that underpin the location of the neighbourhood are made informally. None of the parents shared any concrete research; rather this was achieved through 'grapevine' or 'hot' knowledge (Ball and Vincent 1998), 'open to all but only acted upon by those with economic capital, is socially embedded in networks and localities ... it is contrasted with cold or formal knowledge which is encapsulated in school league tables and examination results' (ibid.).

Escaping the 'ghetto-like' poverty trap

It is an anomaly that most advocates of the self-segregation thesis are quick to point out the cultural manifestations of segregation but fail to cite its destructive socio-economic costs. Self-segregation for Muslims, or clustering of Muslims in one geographical area, is not ideal utopia, neither is it based upon leafy Muslim middle-class suburbia; rather these neighbourhoods are associated with high levels of poverty underpinned by poor social and educational infrastructure, high unemployment or low paid employment and overcrowded housing combined with low productivity. It is these grim social realities which signify the drive that many Muslims have to escape the poverty trap which not only locks families into perpetual failure but also exposes them to the world of drugs and solvent abuse that many Muslims parents have associated with 'ghetto-like' conditions. The opportunities and speed of social mobility, as far as Muslim communities are concerned, are rather slow. For example Platt (2005), in a longitudinal study on migration and social mobility, found evidence in support of the following observation. She noted how some religious groups such as the Jews and Hindus are more likely to end up in higher social groups than their parents, compared with Sikhs and Muslims who have reduced chances of so doing. In light of these socio-economic realities, parents viewed education as a significant route to escaping 'ghetto-like' conditions. Whilst the need and urgency to escape these conditions were felt by all Muslims, the opportunities to escape the poverty trap were only available to a few, particularly those with sufficient economic capital (Bordieu and Passeron 1999) to speed up the process of integration. Two main groups of Muslims were identified as having the financial capital. The first comprised *entrepreneurial Muslims*, Muslim families that were able to develop financial security through business, such as the popular demands of the Indian curry trade or by responding to the growing 'Asian' grocery and poultry market. Whilst accurate figures on the size of the curry trade are difficult to establish, nevertheless the UK curry industry magazine *Spice Business* estimates that the UK curry industry is worth £3.6 billion, with 2.5 million customers eating in any one of 10,000 restaurants (Khaleel 2012). The second group was *erudite Muslims* who are able to use the educational system as a way of exiting the 'ghetto-like' condition of the neighbourhood by getting on to the professional ladder through a combination of economic and cultural capital. For example, between 1991 and 2001 ethnic minority groups in the UK saw an improvement in educational attainments, most significantly the Pakistani group, the most numerous ethnic Muslim group in Britain, which experienced an 18 percentage point increase in degree-level qualification (Lymperopoulou and Parameshwaran 2014). Both of these groups of Muslims are motivated by their desire for social mobility, but also by the recognition that education combined with hard work can bring about liberating experiences (Clark et al. 2007).

Ethnically segregated areas are also socially segregated areas (Dorling 2011), both such neighbourhoods providing few opportunities for their children's social mobility. Segregated state schools in ethnically deprived neighbourhoods provide limited educational opportunities; rather there is a tendency to reproduce socioeconomic forms of deprivation from one generation to the following, thus making it difficult for families to escape or break out of the cycle of deprivation. It is clear from Muslim discourses that those able to move out of deprived neighbourhoods did so with the aim to locate their children in spaces which would expose them to different environments that would allow them to develop the relevant social and cultural capital linked to social mobility. The following observation drawing upon the respondent's personal experiences reinforces the point very clearly.

> I have been living in this area for over three years, it's a nice area all our neighbours are white and we get on well. My kids were growing up and did not want them to grow up in 'crack city'. Things are bad; my children are of that age if I did not move out then they would have been influenced by that. Within my own extended family there are cases that I can talk about. I know the impacts it has on immediate families and also extended families. You can't tie your child at home they would want to go out and play with their friends and you can't watch them all day ... So now I am happy it's a quiet area the kids are at home most of the time in their own rooms on their computer and they go to a good school. This is the main fact, at least now by going to a good school they can make something out of themselves. In many respects I am very fortunate I had the financial ability to move out. I know of other people that want to move out but their financial circumstances are different. In this current financial crisis things are going to get even more difficult.

The socio-economic realities, together with the bleak prospects offered to both parents and their children, does not fit within the neatly bounded construction of self-segregation. It is clear that families living in predominantly Asian areas did not articulate a desire to live 'separately' or maintain a parallel existence; rather, monocultural neighbourhoods were products of poverty and personal circumstances underpinned by the realities of social class positionality. Those who had left their 'ghetto-like' existence were a privileged few who not only had the desire but, more crucially, had the ability to move out, and in doing so they displayed a sense of achievement and accomplishment for their own respective families and the wider community. This is clearly articulated by the following account of social mobility cited below.

You see when I first moved out mainly in search of a good house and also for a better future for my children ... They now attend a very good school. But I think the fact that we have moved has been a positive sign for others, now everyone else would also move. You see when I meet the people where I used to live in our old area, they look at me differently and see my in a different light ... because they know we have made the right move for our children's future ... you see you have to ask yourself who wants to live in the ghetto-like neighbourhood.

The above observations clearly demonstrate how debates on Muslim integration link social class positionalities. For Muslim communities, integration is not a problematic issue, rather it is an experience which is embraced, because it allows families to make use of some of the perks of integration to achieve social mobility through integrated schools. Integrated schools are thus multi-dimensional constructs predicated not only on economic phenomena but also significantly connected with forms of social reproduction and cultural distinction. It confirms the notion that in order for Muslim pupils to do well they have to be exposed to various forms of cultural capital and cultural competencies which are often produced and reproduced through middle-class educational experiences.

Avoiding the racism trap

For those Muslims embracing the 'cultural turn' away from their 'ghetto-like' existence, towards the path of integration, or indeed social mobility, they still have to navigate through the difficult terrains of middle-classness as 'Whiteness' (Archer 2011) and anti-Muslim racism. It has been noted how the minority ethnic middle class/es embody an 'ambivalent structural location that combines both (class) privilege and (racial) exclusion' (ibid.). In addition, Muslim communities have squared the rhetoric of post-racial discourses with the deeply embedded animosity towards Muslims in light of the War on Terror (Miah 2012). They do so through a deeply ambivalent process which aims to balance the desired objectives with the lived realities and fears which are predicated upon the rhetoric associated with the ongoing War on Terror at an international level, combined with the securitised governance of Muslim communities through counter-terrorism and de-radicalisation policies at a local level. Some of these essentialised fears of Muslims are then used to channel anti-Muslim racism within a school context, and this is further confirmed by the following.

> The government is always pushing through new policies on pre-venting extremism targeted at us! You see, the average Joe doesn't know the difference between a good or a bad Muslim. He sees brown skin and he thinks we're all closet terrorists. This is some-thing we have to factor in mind when we choose our schools for our children; we don't want to take our children out from the poverty trap, only to expose them to anti-Muslim racism.

In order to overcome or navigate some of the many cultural politics of schooling, Muslim parents choose to balance the risks against the potential benefits by sending their children to high-achieving ethni-cally mixed schools which provide good education whilst allowing a support structure through group solidarity with fellow Muslims or pupils. This shows how Muslim parents, in addition to considering teaching standards, location, type of school, league tables, pedagogy and class, when choosing a secondary school had to seriously con-sider the politics of racism and anti-Muslim prejudice. They did this to ensure that they did not escape the poverty trap only to expose their children to educational spaces characterised by persistent dis-regard for cultural differences and other forms of school malaises, which Bourdieu has termed *la petite misère*, or ordinary suffering (cited in Dumas 2014). The following account of a Muslim parent in Manchester explores many themes associated with collective social suffering (ibid.) and, in particular, provides clear examples of how Muslim parents deal with racial ambivalence. It further highlights the disconnect associated with dominant racial rhetoric associated with 'post-racism' (Mirza 2010; British Futures 2012) which implies that race and ethnicity are no longer the significant markers they once were for minority ethnic communities and lived Muslim experiences. In fact it seems that concerns relating to racism or anti-Muslim prej-udice are an essential feature for all Muslims regardless of their social economic position in society.

There is also an underlining fear that most Muslims have in sending their children to an all-White school; it's sad, but the reality is
that I couldn't live with knowingly sending my child to a school
that is racist. If my child is the only brown face then he is going
to stick out, it's a perfect target practice! That's way it's important in choosing a mixed school in a good area. We don't want
a school that is 100 per cent Muslim, nor do we want a school
which is all White. It has to be mixed school. For us it's not just
the grade, unlike white middle class parents, we can't move into
any neighbourhoods. Yes the school has to be high achieving –
the neighbourhood and also the school have to be mixed. That is
why white middle class schools are the best – you will get the best
grades.

Integration as social mobility

For Muslim parents, ethnically mixed schools are much sought after,
especially those that are attended by White middle-class pupils.
Ethnically mixed schools provide an ideal route for Muslim parents to escape the poverty trap associated with ethnically segregated schools, while at the same time providing sufficient support
and safety in numbers with fellow Muslim or BME pupils to help
prevent their being singled out for racism. The focus on race, religion and the factor of social class is salient, especially given how
Muslim parents would be reluctant to send their children to schools
with poor White working-class and poor Muslim pupils; this is
usually associated with desired outcomes for social mobility for
their children's futures. Such a viewpoint demonstrates some of
the complexities associated with educational choices and the social
class distinctions made by some Muslim parents. For Muslim parents, exposing their children to an environment which will allow
them to acquire cultural and social capital is vital for the invest-
ment made by the parents to nurture intergenerational progress and
mobility.

Integration for Muslim parents is motivated by utilitarian principles and is grounded upon self-interest; ethnically mixed schools
play a crucial role in ensuring that children are doing well. Some
Muslim parents maintain the view that education in general, and
ethnically mixed schools in particular, with a middle-class bias have

the potential to empower minority ethnic communities with the opportunities associated with social mobility. The question of social mobility is connected with the hope that greater integration will lead to both inter- and intra-generational changes – the former is linked to social mobility between one's family and his/her class and/or social status, whilst the latter refers to one's social class mobility experienced during one's individual career. For Muslim parents, education was seen as key for intergenerational forms of social mobility as this provided positive impacts for their children's future. However, intergenerational changes were determined by intra-generational forms of mobility – because this provided sufficient *capital* which allowed their children to be located in the right catchment area for an appropriate school.

The connections between social mobility and class consciousness are particularly crucial, as they demonstrate the view that upward signs of mobility are associated with the realisation of class as a status group. Thus the movement into middle-class neighbourhoods demonstrates signs of upward mobility in the same way that sending a child to a school outside the majority 'Muslim' community signifies a shift in status. The recognition of class consciousness in shaping educational decision making for primary and secondary schools is a delicate balancing act between race and class, and this is further confirmed by the following research.

A small minority of aspirant Black and Asian parents actively avoided schools that were Black/Asian majority, engaging, where affordable, in high rates of residential and educational flight, despite their own awareness of risks associated with educating their children in predominantly white schools.

(Weekes-Bernard 2007:41)

Conclusion

The above observation demonstrates how the one-dimensional framing of Muslim self-segregation does not reflect the lived reality of Muslim experience. Popular and policy discourses on Muslims in state schools, as highlighted in chapters 1, 2 and 3, fail to recognise the intersectional discursive realities based upon faith, race and social class in determining parental choice of school, with mixed schools seen as ideal spaces for schooling. Muslim parental choice is not an instrument of ethnic separatism; rather it is a complex intersectional process between race, class and faith.

Ideas if spatial and cultural self-segregation used to describe Muslim communities are contested within this chapter; it seems that the energy and priority for Muslim communities lie more in social mobility and integration then in cultivating parallel lives. The chapter has demonstrated how class consciousness and levels of *parentocracy* (Brown 1994) of Muslim parents allows mixed schools within affluent 'middle-class' areas to be considered as the most popular school choice; this is based upon a perception that integration or living in an integrated mixed community is one of the principal pathways for Black and minority communities to escape concentrated poverty which is characterised by urban disorder, vandalism and antisocial behaviour.

Parental accounts of integration drew parallels between residential integration and choice of school; integration within this context focused on the desire to move into affluent, leafy suburbia as a way of positioning themselves for better social mobility. This is perhaps key to the framing of integration through the context of equality in pursuing the meritocratic ideal; Muslim parents buy into the notion that, through the process of integration, status is acquired through ability and merit. It further recognises that, under certain circumstances, the existence of integrated schools is largely determined by the parents' economic and cultural capital. One of the main drivers of integration for Muslim parents is based upon the socio-economic benefits associated with education and intergenerational mobility. The crucial point to note is that Muslim parents do not escape 'inequality-producing segregation' through recreating Muslim middle-class suburbia, as in some African-American middle-class enclaves (Cashin 2004), but rather by attempting to integrate with the middle-class host society.

This chapter shows that *some* Muslim parents, empowered through their economic capital, not only desire but actively pursue the course of integration, and this recognition and affirmation of integration is an important mechanism through which status is gained within the community. It shows how Muslim communities are not static communities, but rather are best described as shifting geographies of ethnic settlement symbolised by movement out of traditional areas into more mixed and diverse neighbourhoods. In other words some Muslim communities actively pursue integration, initially through residential followed by educational integration because, according to the experiences of Muslim parents, school segregation is directly related to residential segregation.

6
Paradoxes of Muslim Faith Schools

> Just because we attend a Muslim faith school this does not make us less British. In the same way that Muslims attending state schools makes them less Muslim.
>
> (Year 10 Muslim Girl)

> To Abdullah Trevathan, head teacher of north London's Islamia School, a state-funded school that offers religious instruction and the study of Arabic along with the standard national curriculum, the answer is clear. Trevathan believes that schools such as Islamia – one of the schools to receive state funding in Britain – can play a vital role in hammering out a new Muslim identity, one that combines being a good Muslim with being a good citizen in a pluralist society.
>
> (Jay 2005:37)

Faith schools in general are often seen through negative lenses within popular discourse; this is evident from the opposition and critical reception they receive from a number of secular agencies, such as the British Humanist Association (BHA), and also from faith-based coalition groups such as the Accord Coalition. In recent years it has been Muslim faith schools, which critics claim is established with the sole aim of preserving Muslim cultural identity, that have received the bulk of the antagonism regarding self-segregation. In fact, prior to the Trojan Horse stories, which hit the national media in March 2014, it was the Al-Madinah School in Derby that was the topic and focus of much debate and discussion within public and policy circles during later part of 2013. It opened as a Muslim faith school under the government's flagship education programme of Free Schools. Free Schools are independent schools, free from local government control or interference; they are similar to school academies in that they are run by a non-profit charitable trust. Al-Madinah School, an all-through school which combines both primary and secondary provision, opened in 2012 as part of the government's second wave of Free Schools. In September 2013 news started to emerge that Al-Madinah School was 'imposing strict Islamic practices' on both pupils and staff, including non-Muslims being required to sign new contracts forcing them to wear the hijab. There were also suggestions that boys were receiving preferential treatment over girls (Bains and Spencer 2013). In response to these concerns the school was inspected by Ofsted, which raised a number of serious concerns relating to health and safety, school governance and poor-quality teaching. Ironically, the inspectors had little to say about the popular discussion relating to the school's practice of promoting cultural separatism (Ofsted 2013). In light of the Ofsted inspection, Lord Nash, Parliamentary Under-secretary for State Schools, wrote to Al-Madinah School on 8 October 2014 giving the school the opportunity to improve, whilst at the same time seeking written confirmation that the school was following equality legislation regarding the alleged unfair treatment of girls within the school (DoE 2013). Following an Ofsted monitoring inspection in December 2014, Lord Nash announced that the school had failed to make significant changes and, as a result, the secondary tier of Al-Madinah School was closed (DoE 2014).

The Al-Madinah School debate symbolises a schooling practice which is the antithesis of Western secular liberalism, and it also highlights the cultural practices of Muslim schools which have made conscious attempts to create and maintain segregation. These ideas of cultural segregation often revolve around the perception of gender segregation and the unfair treatment of girls and privileging of boys according to school policies and practices. Some of the concerns in regard to gender segregation are rooted in a long tradition of policy and academic debates; this will be the focus of the first section of this chapter. The second part of the chapter offers a critical analysis of self-segregation in light of interviews and focus group meetings with Muslim girls attending faith schools in Britain, and also with Muslim parents who had decided to send their children to Muslim faith schools. It will provide a counter-narrative to the popular debate on faith schools through the prism of segregation by demonstrating how Muslim pupils favour an agency approach rather than a structural interpretation of Muslim faith schools. It will further demonstrate how Muslim pupils are free and critical agents, defining and redefining their social experiences in light of the debate on integration and segregation. In doing so, Muslim pupils rupture the binary position of the integration debate by suggesting how faith schools can provide students with the skills and ability to interact with secularism and Britishness through the application of a double critique (Safi 2003) of both the traditional Muslim interpretation of Islam and the debates around muscular liberalism (Cameron 2011a).

Self-segregation through faith schools

Muslim schools are to 'ban our culture' (Hall 2009) and 'Muslim Schools cause segregation' (*Daily Mail* 2008) were among the headlines in the British press which has fuelled popular fear and backlash of Muslim faith schools. These popular fears are often constructed within the socio-political background of counter-terrorism and Muslim radicalism. As already noted in Chapter 1, the recent emphasis on counter-terrorism is focused not only on violent extremism but also on non-violent extremism which, if unchallenged, can lead to a slippery slope towards violent extremism (Cameron 2011a). Some have argued that principles of cultural diversity in general and Muslim culture in particular are antithetical to liberal values and customs, and as a result greater emphasis should be placed upon the pursuit of an ideal form of life, or a life based upon liberalism, which above all is non-negotiable (ibid.). It is within this spirit that Muslim schools are often viewed through the prism of divisiveness segregation and counter-liberalism (Short 2002; Merry 2005; McCreary et al. 2007; Odone 2008; Halstead 2009). Since the events of 9/11 and, more importantly, the London bombings of 7/7, Muslim schools have often been seen as incubators of extremism, and the reaction to fundamentalism has shaped the popular discourse with regard to Muslim faith schools. Some of these fears over Muslim faith schools have a long history of perceived sectarian institutions, nurturing 'separatist beliefs' with a view to maintaining and sustaining culturally detached institutions (Grillo 1998). The educational content

and values of Muslim faith schools were also seen as deeply problematic. For example, David Bell the then chief Inspector of Schools
and head of the Ofsted, perceived Muslim schools to be undermining
the process of equipping Muslim students for life in modern Britain
(Smithers 2005). The 'strict' gender segregation of girls from the age
of puberty, seen as one of the popular drivers for Muslim schools, has
also attracted considerable criticism (Afshar 1989; Haw 1994; Basit
1997). Gender segregation is interpreted as a medium through which
segregation of culture and the patriarchal control by Muslim men
over Muslim women is achieved and sustained. Thus it is not surprising to note that the role of Muslim faith schools has come to be seen
to define Muslim women as potential moral and cultural anchors
(Afshar 1989). The debate arising from Al-Madinah School suggests
that British Muslims socialise their 'daughters to construct a British
identity by adopting and rejecting aspects...of British ethnicities
through a combination of freedom and control' (Basit 1997:425).
Furthermore, the public debates seem to give credence to centre-
Right critiques of Muslim communities, arguing that they are defined
in opposition to the liberal West and also pose challenges 'to our
own educational beliefs and values' (McCreary et al. 2007:203). The
above sentiments are crystallised by the centre-Right, London-based
think tank Civitas, which sees Muslim faith schools as part of a
broader social problem by their rejection of integration and placing
great emphasis on differences between, desertion of and resistance to
Western influences.

> Non-Muslim countries as part of the realm of unbelief and they
> see education as a process of inoculating children against infec-
> tion by Western ideas. As far as possible they try to shield children
> from Western influence – hence the prohibition of art, music, and
> drama – but above all children are taught to reject the Western
> tradition of learning through discussion and argument.
>
> (MacEoin 2009:9)

Moreover the above report, echoing the popular discourse on Muslim
faith schools, highlights three possible consequences which could
result from this 'cultural sectarianism' of Muslim communities. First,
it argues that Muslim pupils are not taught to be active citizens
in the country they live in. Second, it maintains that children are

actively taught to reject mainstream British culture, which could make pupils more vulnerable to some of the messages of violent extremism. Finally, it stresses that this neo-cultural separatism could undermine the 'religious toleration that has been the hallmark of this country for many years' (ibid.). To sum up, Muslim schools are seen as defining a cultural space which is grounded upon extended family honour and loyalty to religious tradition, which is seen to be in opposition to Western secular liberalism (Merry 2005; McCreary et al. 2007).

Integration and not segregation through faith

Most of the criticism associated with Muslim faith schools has focused on its institutional concerns whether it be the curriculum, ethos, governance or gender composition. Very few studies have actually engaged pupils on their experiences on Muslim faith schools in light of the question of segregation and integration.

Based on empirical data, this section aims to highlight the clear disconnect between the policy framing of Muslim schools and the reality as understood by Muslim pupils. In complete contrast to the idea of Muslim schools nurturing social and cultural isolation, Muslim pupils attending Muslim girls' schools felt that Muslim schools provided a dialectical space which nurtured a sense of Britishness grounded upon the construct of British Muslim identity – an identity nurtured by the social and cultural landscape of Britain. It demonstrates how, by attending a Muslim faith school, they were able to question and discuss contemporary ideas associated with integration, segregation and identity, something which fellow Muslim pupils in state schools took as granted. Moreover, it was clear that issues associated with citizenship, integration and community cohesion were extensively discussed during and outside the school hours.

The subsequent observations noted below establish one of the ways in which integration is discussed by students attending Muslim faith schools. They provide a critique of the popular understanding of Muslim faith schools as spaces of 'fixity' or unchanging boundaries of identity construct. Instead, the following discussion confirms wider research on Muslim faith schools as spaces where a British Muslim identity is constructed (Meer 2010) based upon the mutual compatibility of faith and national identity (Mogahed and Nyri 2007). The focus group respondents verify how an idea of faith and nationality nurtures their own self-construct. In light of this, it was not surprising to find the focus group members displaying a very strong sense of British Muslim identity, which was informed by the socio-cultural environment of the schools they attended. The critical point questioned by the pupil below is the linear relationship between school and identity through blurring of the categories between schooling, faith and nationality.

> If someone asks us how to define our self, we say that we are British Muslims. That is the way it has been installed in us and that's the way we define ourselves. Just because we attend a Muslim faith school this does not make us less British. In the same way that Muslims attending state schools makes them less Muslim.

British Muslim identity was a major theme that was consistent throughout the Muslim faith school focus group. For the Muslim girls, religion was determined by one's spirituality and the way in which one conducts one's affairs within society. Britishness is largely determined by the place of one's birth, the geographical location where one lives and the probity of the individual. Both of these issues, namely religion and nationality, were mutually compatible and each played a symbiotic role in influencing the other, in the same way that religion and nationality in Muslim majority countries help define the cultural manifestations of Islam. In light of this observation, Muslim pupils felt that to live out a British Muslim identity was seen as a liberating experience. Many saw the impacts of socio-cultural surroundings as playing a crucial role in them becoming 'true Muslims'. Being a 'true Muslim' involves having a pristine identity which recognises the importance of location (Al-Alwani 2003; Abdullah 2004) in shaping ethnicity. It was argued that 'Pakistani' or 'Indian Islam' in Britain was largely mediated through the ethnic markers of the respective countries; thus, intermarriage between various castes or ethnic groups was largely prohibited or socially frowned upon. A British Muslim identity, the girls argued, has the ability to transcend these cultural markers and allow Muslims to practise their faith. As one of the focus group members noted:

> I think it's generally how you live your life, you can either live it as a true Muslim or you can just call yourself a Muslim.

British Islam has the potential for nurturing a 'true Muslim' identity: an identity which is interested in the way faith is practised in its 'ideal form' and not one that is mediated by kinship-based politics. These cultural practices, based upon kinship, were seen as antithetical to the generic principles of Islam: 'true Islam', it was argued, comes as a result of expansion of religious knowledge which transcends the Indian subcontinental frame of reference. An example of this is based upon the idea of valuing freedom of religious practice or the importance of greater individual autonomy in defining the British Muslim experience. This particular framing of Muslim identity is essentially a generational phenomenon, with new and merging Muslim communities drawing upon the diasporic cultural reference to articulate their worldview (Kalra et al. 2005). This is clearly articulated in the following observation.

> I think as younger generation we are freer and we let others be free. You see the older generation have strict ideas, such as Pakistani can't marry an Indian. It was looked down upon, but now I think things will change with the new generation, we are more accommodating and accepting. I think our parents also realise this, as British Muslims we do things differently.

The above discussion shows how the Muslim girls view themselves as autonomous agents of change, with an active independent voice or, in the words of the above respondent, 'as British Muslims we do things differently'. Greater religious autonomy was seen as an important feature of the British Muslim identity, this being understood through the rupturing of religious identity shaped by the geographical location from which their parents or grandparents had migrated. Muslim pupils used a number of repertoires to explore this idea. For example, some pushed for an ecumenical framing of Islam which recognises the importance of unity and cooperation *within* the Muslim communities and a greater alliance and collaboration *between* faiths. One of the principle areas of religious autonomy focused on the way in which marriage, romance and relationship was debated. Marriage was framed within a broader Islamic framework; the fact that Islam places no prohibition on people taking marriage partners of different nationalities or ethnicities was seen as an empowering force. In light of this, Muslim pupils acknowledged the shift in the

conceptualisation of marriage between the first and second generation of Muslim communities, with the former focusing more on
endogamy and the latter exploring the wider possibilities of romantic
love as a way of finding marriage partners, which can often transcend
one's ethnic group.

The Muslim girls felt that their faith school experience 'installed'
a positive self-image which in turn nurtured a British Muslim identity. They argued that this was vital, especially because it was seen to
provide an ideal springboard to the wider society. The discourse on
integration revealed an open attitude to the wider society whereby
secular space was not seen to be in conflict with the teachings
of Islam; rather, it was a space where Muslims can negotiate and
also make positive contributions. The overall narrative showed how
attending a Muslim faith school was not a means to an end, rather
a transitional sojourn; once completed it would provide relevant
and necessary skills for the future. Furthermore, it demonstrated
that faith school education instilled discipline, good manners and
strong ethics, all vital components for good citizens. This is articulated in the subsequent observation, which rejects the popular
notion that attending Muslim faith school can be a barrier to future
integration.

> I don't think it's going to be an issue going to college, univer-
> sity or even work. I think coming to this school has given us a
> lot emotionally, morally and ethically. It has taught us not only
> to be good Muslims but also to be good human beings and good
> citizens. Also, it has taught us the importance of interacting with
> other people but also how to interact with wider society. I think it
> has been beneficial coming to a faith school as this one, as it really
> prepares you for the big wide world.

The idea that faith schools promote cultural segregation was challenged by Muslim pupils; rather they viewed their experience of
schooling through the prism of integration as a positive act and a naturally occurring process, whereby migrant communities go through
a process of social and cultural change. As already noted above,
British Muslim identity recognised the importance of diverse ways
of imagining Britishness and the centrality of faith within public
space (Modood 2007). They also appreciated the need of pragmatism

in that it recognised that some give and take is required for active citizenship in a multicultural society.

Whilst there was criticism of the traditional form of Muslim practice located within a different cultural landscape when applied within Britain, equally there was criticism of policies which attempted to enforce assimilation. This *double critique* (Safi 2003) is clear from the reservations which indicated attempts to politicise the idea of integration as a way of undermining religious identity. There is a general criticism that, whilst social and cultural change was a normative experience within the Muslim community, particularly amongst young people, it was felt that there was little or no recognition of this within public discourse. One of the reasons for this was the fact that some political actors wanted to use the idea of integration in pursuing assimilation for political gain by wanting Muslims to abandon their religious identity and embrace a secular worldview; under such circumstances it was argued that this form of 'integration', which was politically and ideologically motivated, should be resisted. The above observation demonstrates how Muslim girls are involved in discursive negotiation between preserving core religious identity and interacting with wider secular space.

> Muslims do integrate, but what do they want us to do, do they want us to do un-Islamic activities? We can't do that, as she says, we have to develop a barrier of resistance. There are things that we can or want to do and there are things which we don't want to do. You can't force people; we don't go around telling other people what to do and not to do. We just let people be, even though we may disagree with it.

British Muslim identity and Muslim faith schools

Muslim faith schools are often criticised for providing an education for Muslims in an enclosed environment away from contacts or interaction with people of different faiths. It is argued that these highly controlled environments provide a space which not only 'protects' Muslims pupils from 'western' lifestyles, but also results in Muslims despising mainstream British culture (MacEoin 2009; Gilligan 2010). Following this logic, one would have thought that Muslims attending Muslim faith schools would have demonstrated strong animosity or even hatred towards British secular society, but in fact the complete opposite is closer to reality. For young Muslims, essentialised Muslimness is not the sole category which reflects their self-concept but rather a hyphenated British Muslim identity (Ramadan 2009a), which is grounded in the cultural land-scape of Britain that draws on both Muslim and secular ideas of tolerance, acceptance and respect. This viewpoint constructed their own approach to *modus vivendi* (Gray 2000) in their search for com-mon ground between different and often competing approaches to diversity.

A British Muslim identity based upon an 'ideal type' construct, free from any denominational links or ties – or more importantly linked to traditional societies from which their parents migrated – constitutes young people's worldview. For most young people it is important to live their lives according to *true Islam*, which is grounded in the idea of tolerance, objectivity and conviviality. In this context, 'Muslimness' is very much defined through an ecumenical visioning which transcends nationalistic or other 'clan-based' link-age. In traditional Muslim societies, marriage is usually arranged by parents and mutually agreed by both the bride and groom. In most, if not all the cases, marriages would be arranged within the same ethnic group or within the same clan, family or tribe. These cases of endogamy are seen as prime examples of the continuation of tra-ditional practices which reinforce self-segregation. For example, the 2001 UK Census data highlighted how 96 per cent of Muslim women married within their own faith. Moreover, levels of first-cousin mar-riages within communities in Bradford and Birmingham were seen as sustaining high levels of endogamy and homogamy – it is estimated that at least 55 per cent of British Pakistani couples are first cousins (Peach 2006). British Muslimness is positioned in stark contrast to the practice of endogamy, and it is not surprising to note that Muslim girls were very much in support of marriages across ethnic groups – providing they shared the same faith. This, they were quick to high-light, was a significant shift from their parents' attitudes. Moreover, the girls felt that *group* solidarity based upon tribal loyalties to a single ethnic group was essentially wrong and should be resisted.

For British Muslims, traditional practices of Islam mediated either through the traditional practices of *Berelawi* (Metcalf 2002) or *Deobandi* (Sikand 2002), which are often conservative visions of

Muslim devotion rooted in the historical and socio-cultural landscape of the Indian subcontinent, seem to offer very little prospects for Muslims in the West. In fact pupils attending Muslim faith schools managed and funded by *Deobandi* and *Berelawi* communities did little to inspire their worldview. Whilst these traditional educational infrastructures played a crucial role in their understanding of Muslim text and aspects of Islamic worship, in regard to dealing with fellow Muslims or indeed wider society they projected an ecumenical spirit of Islam based upon individual autonomy and a greater pluralistic encompassing vision of Islam. In doing so, the Muslim girls were not only rejecting the Muslim cultural frame of reference imported by their parents and sustained by the community, but were also developing their own frame of reference for religious and cultural practice. In short, Muslim young people were able to contextualise faith within the socio-cultural context of Britain. The following observation confirms this position, demonstrating how Muslim pupils might attend a school of a particular denomination, but may have their own agency and own way of defining their Muslimness – this is a very crucial point to note, as it demonstrates that Muslim young girls are not cultural dupes, wilfully and uncritically accepting what is passed to them, but rather shows how they have a good critical consciousness which has the ability to filter what they have been taught in light of their experiences.

> I do not believe in those classifications such as Deobandi etc. Because I think people have the right to believe in what they have to. Some of it might be, or some might say, is wrong, but you can't stop someone believing in something, if that is what they want to believe. I think we should be more open and tolerant. Someone once told me that in Islam, the differences of opinion is a sign of mercy from Allah.

Muslim faith schools and integration: nurturing cultural identity

The intersectional nature of the Muslim discourse on integration was a dominant theme highlighted in the above observations. Muslim communities realised the importance of the cultural recognition of one's religious identity within the public domain, identity not being viewed as something which should be kept within the private domain; rather, they recognised the role that identity can play in the process of integration. Parents felt that a child needs to have a strong cultural identity; this, they feel, will allow the child to have a strong foundation, confidence and motivation for the future. If students are deprived of this learning, it is argued, they will experience ambivalence towards their own heritage and also the overall values of British society. An educational system which nurtures a person's cultural identity will help facilitate the process of integration and active citizenship. The importance of recognising this distinction is summarised below.

> When you drive around the streets in Burnley you see all the plastic gangsters thinking that they are part of some hip hop movie. It is very worrying! They have no sense of self or any direction that is why they're behaving in the manner that they do. It is clear that if these children had a strong sense of self or the schools provided a good foundation about their religion – this would help them…I can give you so many examples of how children that live in this area with good knowledge of religion are making positive contributions through voluntary work. I believe that a strong sense of self helps you go places. I am a simple person but I'm sure if you look you will find evidence for this. That is why I don't object to parents sending kids to Muslim schools because at least they get to learn good manners and have a positive identity.

The above observations summarised the objective behind why some parents choose a faith school for their children – it was clear that parents had a broader educational perspective in mind, that they recognised the importance education played not only in achieving economic goals, but also in developing and nurturing good character. Parents did not wish to send their child to Muslim faith schools to maintain a separate or parallel life; rather, they felt it would facilitate the process of integration through good character. In order to maintain the balance between religious obligation, character building and collective civic duty, some parents sent their girls to a Muslim faith school during the day and then to the Brownies, which is a church-based Girl Scout organisation, in the evening. The following examples summarise the complex issues that some Muslim parents have to juggle, whilst also considering the broad and holistic education of children.

> We have a young daughter and we have placed her in an Islamic school, this decision was not easy we thought about it long and hard. So it was difficult, the area that we live is all-white. In this school she attends is 100 per cent Muslim but the thing is that there are children from different cultural backgrounds such as Algerian, Arab, Pakistani, and Bangladeshi etc. So she has a very strong sense of the Muslim identity, and I think that is important for her future, but we realised that this did not do anything in the short term as far as getting to know the wider community. After a long thought we decided to send her to the Brownies so that she gets the integration. This has been our rational choice; this we feel gives her full experience of diverse Muslim communities and also the local non-Muslim community.

The above observation also highlights an additional dilemma facing some Muslim parents, which is the importance of Muslim children developing a good understanding of the internal diversity of the Muslim community which covers the experiences of the global Muslim nations, while at the same time recognising the importance of understanding the local non-Muslim community. It is clear from the above observation that the question of diversity plays an important part in the wider thought process of educational upbringing. It also rejects the idea that Muslim parents self-consciously use faith schools for self-segregation; in doing so it ruptures the binary construct of the integration-versus-segregation debate of Muslim faith schools. The importance of recognising one's cultural difference as a way of directing positive future prospects is further highlighted in the following example, by drawing upon the respondent's family experiences and how sending their child to a Muslim girls' school achieved more for the process of integration through nurturing positive self-confidence.

> My brother sent their children to the Muslim girl's school which did not have a sixth form college. So he sent them to local Sixth Form College. They did not experience any problems in integrating with the non-Muslim students. We are hoping by sending our

daughter to the same Muslim school and also the same Sixth Form College, hopefully our daughter would do the same. We think that this strategy will work with our own daughter. This has been the upbringing of my father. He taught us and I always take this principle with me. Always make sure that you have a strong sense of who you are, but at the same time do your best to integrate with the wider society. One of the main reasons why my brother and I have decided to send our children to Muslim faith school is not to be separate instead we feel that having a good sense of who you are helps you connect and integrate with British society.

The above principle of sending children to Muslim faith school is based upon the idea that this will help them integrate into wider society, with the view that faith schools enhance pupils' educational attainment, self-esteem and sense of cultural identity and that the result of such enhancement helps to strengthen inter-communal ties (Short 2002). In the case highlighted below, further evidence can also be seen to emerge in support of the above argument. In this case a parent contrasts his experience of sending his son to the Manchester Muslim School for Boys with that of students who attended mixed state schools in Oldham. He feels that sending his child to a Muslim faith school has done more for integration and cross-cultural contact than state schools in Oldham.

In Oldham there is clear evidence of segregation, look at the schools also the neighbourhood, it won't take you long to figure that out. I have only one child. But we decided to send him to the Muslim Boys School in Manchester. I tell you it was not that easy – I drove him down every day and picked him up. This was a good experience he was able to learn and have a good understanding of his faith. More importantly he had the chance to mix with different Muslims from different parts of the world such as Arabs, and White Muslims etc. He would not have had that chance to meet with these types of people living in Oldham. Now he is at the Sixth Form College he has a mixed set of friends mainly white kids. Compare that with the other Pakistani and Bangladeshi kids they all stick together. So I feel that the experience of attending a Muslim faith school did him a world of good. The question is all the other Muslim kids went to either to a school with 100 per cent

Asians or a mixed school yet they still stick together. I think my son's experience has helped him integrate into Britain.

Both of the above observations demonstrate the importance of framing Muslim faith schools not as a separatist discourse but rather as an experience that will help children integrate in the future. This idea of faith schools as institutions that delay the process of integration is an important and crucial theme that was highlighted by a number of parents. Moreover, the importance of 'seeing' how this process works within immediate and extended families provides a useful route for parents who are concerned about the cultural and religious identity of their child while at the same time are conscious about the importance of integration. The fact that none of the faith schools within the Manchester area is voluntary-aided or grant-maintained means that parents who want to use the idea of 'delayed integration' (Meer 2007) can only do so if they have the financial means. Many parents expressed an interest in the option of sending their child to a Muslim school, but financial circumstances and the number of children in the household meant that the option of sending all of their children was not realistic or viable financially.

Conclusion

In light of some of the key questions relating to Muslims in Britain, Muslim faith schools pose a number of challenges for politicians and educational policy officials. Some of these questions relate to the big questions concerning the nature of all faith schools, whilst other questions relate to the Muslim faith in particular. The current debate over Muslim faith schools symbolises school practices which are the antithesis to Western secular liberalism, and it also highlights the cultural practices of some Muslim schools that have made conscious attempts to create and maintain segregation.

The question of gender segregation in Muslim faith schools usually revolves around the premise that Muslim communities use Muslim girls' schools as a medium for cultural self-segregation. Within the broader context of this debate, Muslim girls are viewed as victims of cultural oppression, whose sole objective in schooling is to preserve 'antiquated cultural values' – thus undermining the ideas of 'Britishness'. In response to this question, this chapter has argued that Muslim girls are not passive subjects, but rather active agents of change. Contrary to popular debate, Muslim experiences question the cultural determinism of Muslim faith schools through an agency approach, demonstrating that Muslim girls are not simply cultural dupes but rather are free critical agents defining and redefining their social experiences in light of the debate on integration and segregation.

The identity formation of pupils within Muslim faith schools problematises contemporary debates on self-segregation and, in doing so, it ruptures the simplistic binary constructs of the integration-versus-segregation debate by suggesting how faith schools can provide students with the skills and ability to interact with secularism and Britishness through an application of a *double critique* of both the Muslim traditional interpretation of Islam and the debates around secular muscular liberalism.

In light of the evidence provided within this chapter, it is argued that some Muslim faith schools can be seen to be consistent with the key tenants of multiculturalism, liberal democracy and communitarian notions of citizenship. It shows, in light of pupil experiences, that tensions arising from the demands of the secular state and obligations of Islam are usually dealt with in a dialectical experience. It sees Muslim identity not as essentialised and unchanging, but rather as part of an experience that is constantly in a state of flux – thus Muslim identity is something which is constantly in the process of evolving (Hall 1992). The British Muslim identity is part of an emerging identity grounded upon independence and creativity which has the ability to balance textual demands with contextual realities – and thus the integration of Muslim communities is not a passive act of conformity to existing cultural norms and values but rather a positive and dynamic entity which contributes to 'building a new Europe' (El-Effendi 2009). In doing so, Muslim communities in Britain are helping to shape a distinctive British identity grounded in the cultural imperative of Islam, which is succinctly summarised below.

> For centuries, Islamic civilization harmonized indigenous forms of cultural expression with the universal norms of its sacred law. It struck a balance between temporal beauty and ageless truth and fanned a brilliant peacock's tail of unity in diversity from the

heart of China to the shores of the Atlantic. Islamic jurisprudence helped facilitate this creative genius. In history, Islam showed itself to be culturally friendly and, in that regard, has been likened to a crystal clear river. Its waters (Islam) are pure, sweet, and life-giving but – having no color of their own – reflect the bedrock (indigenous culture) over which they flow. In China, Islam looked Chinese; in Mali, it looked African. Sustained cultural relevance to distinct peoples, diverse places, and different times underlay Islam's long success as a global civilization.

(Abdullah 2004:1)

7
Poverty, Inequality and Self-Segregation

> Why would Muslim parents intentionally want to send their children to failing schools in deprived neighbourhoods? This self-segregation argument has never made any sense; the real question isn't self-segregation but rather poverty!

The above observation by a Muslim parent, born and educated in Britain, summarises some of the underlining problems associated with the debates on integration and segregation. Most of the analysis on segregation has focused principally on culture and religion as a way of understanding and explaining levels of segregation within neighbourhoods and schools. Instead, what the above parent has succinctly argued is that levels of segregation are best explained as 'inequality-producing segregation' (Merry 2012) – in other words, that it is social circumstances that are producing segregation and not the conscious attempts made by the people in question. One of the ways in which levels of segregation within schools and neighbourhoods are best understood is via poverty, marginalisation and social inequality – and not through the political rhetoric around self-segregation, Britishness and counter-terrorism.

Contemporary discourses on education policy and Muslim communities have focused more on 'culture' than on the equality debate. The issue of Muslims and schooling is not framed within the *distributive justice* paradigm (Rawls 1999); rather, it is viewed through the rhetoric of the racial state, which sees minority communities in general and Muslim communities in particular as problems that need to be addressed (Goldberg 2002). As noted in chapters 1 and 2, concern has been expressed about Muslim culture rather than about socio-economic equality and the politics of equal opportunity and equal outcomes. The debates on self-segregation as the Muslim problematic have taken shape within significant global and local events which have a bearing upon the question of social inequality. First, the policy debates on Muslims have taken place since the Global Financial Crisis of 2007–2008, which has been compared to the Great Depression of the 1930s. This crisis has had serious economic and political repercussions, with a number of banks, such as the Royal Bank of Scotland, Lloyds TSB and Northern Rock Building Society partially nationalised. Second, the impacts of the crisis have led to the politics and policy of austerity; the subsequent election of the Tory-led coalition government in 2010 introduced radical measures to welfare benefits, making it more difficult for people to obtain them, and imposed restrictions on those already on benefits. The coalition's impact on welfare benefits has pushed 1.75 million people in the poorest households deeper into poverty, leaving families struggling to afford basic necessities such as food and energy (Allen 2014). Third, concerns over poverty in Britain saw faith leaders, including 40 Anglican bishops and 600 church leaders, sign a letter calling on political leaders to tackle the causes of food poverty (Butler 2014). This coincided with the publication of a key report by the Trussell Trust, one of the leading organisations providing food banks throughout the UK, which highlighted an increase of 163 per cent in the distribution of food parcels, with more than 900,000 receiving these in 2013–2014 (ibid.). Responding to these concerns, the Muslim communities have also made use of mosques and community centres in Birmingham, Blackburn and Leicester to distribute food parcels to the poor and destitute. More widely coordinated work has also been conducted by the Sufra food bank in London (Forrest 2014).

The framing of Muslims through the pathological lens of cultural determinism rather than through poverty and inequality is particularly ironic, especially in light of the national debate on food poverty, rising cost of living, drastic welfare cuts and lower wages. This irony is particularly stark when levels of poverty are higher amongst Black and minority ethnic communities compared with the majority white population, or when you note that particular Muslim communities, such as the Bangladeshis, show recurring patterns of social inequality; they 'have the lowest income inequality and are consistently the worst off. They have [the] highest poverty rates of all groups and only 25 per cent have incomes that are among the top half of incomes overall' (Barnard and Turner 2011).

The previous chapters has drawn links between social class and integration. Following the same line of inquiry, this chapter demonstrates links between poverty, social inequality and segregation. In doing so it challenges the self-segregation thesis. In many respects Britain is de facto a segregated country determined by high levels of social inequality and social exclusion (Dorling 2011). It seems that deeper concerns relating to poverty within Muslim communities are masked by a debate which prioritises culturally deterministic arguments of self-segregation over social class. This chapter continues some of the themes highlighted in the previous chapters by arguing against the idea of self-segregation and using both Muslim parental and pupil discourses to problematise the binary construct of integration and segregation. It highlights how Muslim communities frame conversations around integration, not by supporting the dominant political rhetoric of integration, but rather through the prisms of racial inequality, fairness and justice (Anderson 2010). In doing so, Muslim parents, whilst recognising the importance of cultural identity, present a more pressing case for distributive justice. It is made clear how some Muslim communities feel that too much emphasis on 'Muslim culture' has tended to mask and undermine more pressing needs and concerns regarding poverty. Moreover, whilst public discourse may not view Muslim communities through social class, class positionalities are an important signifier for the debate on integration and segregation.

Good parent, poor citizen

Parental choice and schooling have been at the centre of educational policy in Britain since the 1944 Education Act. The neighbourhood-based system of schooling, whereby pupils attend their local schools, has been replaced with a 'choice-based' system by the entire political spectrum in Britain. Those advocating parental choice in education normally use the human rights arguments in defence of greater choice. In terms of the human rights aspect, many cite the following clause of the Universal Declaration of Human Rights (UDHR) as a compelling argument in support of parental choice: 'Parents have a prior right to choose the kind of education that shall be given to their children (26, 3).' This argument for parental choice is also prominent in neo-liberal notions of education. It is used to demonstrate how the free market approach to schooling would improve is quality – it is argued that greater competition for places between schools will improve the overall quality and standards in education. Moreover, it is argued that greater choice will allow parents to choose schools which cater for the educational and pedagogical needs of their children.

It is often thought that the choices of Muslim parents may go against the needs of the state by increasing faith or racial segregation (Halstead 1994). This dominant argument that is often used against the Muslim community, that increased parental choice will lead to greater social or ethnic segregation, has been described as the 'good parent, bad citizen' paradox (West 1994). In reality, as argued by a Muslim parent living in Oldham and highlighted below, the best way to approach this paradox is through 'good parent, poor citizen'. Given that most Muslims families live in deprived neighbourhoods, it seems that Muslim parents have very little or no choice in determining their children's educational future, especially given that the element of choice with educational discourse is predicated by social class. To argue that Muslim parents use parental choice to self-segregate, therefore, doesn't reflect the complex realities of Muslim neighbourhoods as it fails to recognise the impacts of racial and ethnic disadvantage.

> If the people that live in this neighbourhood or send their kids at the local school were privileged then they wouldn't have been restricted, they would have sent their children to good schools and lived in good neighbourhoods. But we have to see that the reality is different. We can't afford to move into good areas to get our kids in the best schools, the Christian schools won't accept our kids, we can't blame them; you have to be a Christian. Neither can we afford to send the kids by bus. So it works well for me to send them to the local school which is 90 per cent Muslim ... what choice do I have?

It has long been established by academics that parental choice and schooling is a complicated phenomenon based upon a range of issues such as social capital, selection process and availability. However, this complex approach is seldom applied to exploring and understanding the levels of ethnic segregation within some schools. Instead, it is argued, Muslim parents reinforce ethnic school segregation based upon the desire for self-segregation according to racial or cultural preferences. Among arguments relating to the racialisation of space grounded upon the choices made by Muslim parents relating to Muslim faith schools, some of these accusations are also levelled against Muslim pupils attending segregated state schools.

The problem once again lies within the disconnect between the popular rhetoric on segregation and the lived realities of Muslim communities as noted in the above parental observation. The Muslim discourse on parental choice of schooling demonstrates an awareness of the complex picture governing school choice by questioning the causal relationship between choice and school allocation. It recognises how certain groups in society, due to their socio-economic position, were unable to exercise full choice but rather accepted that when it came to parental choice they had *restricted choice*. Restricted choice recognises that an expression of preference for a particular school is predicated upon a number of variables determined by personal circumstances or external factors. Firstly, this may imply making a restricted choice between various failing state-maintained schools, which are often undersubscribed, within their immediate locality. Secondly, parents may be restricted, due to their cultural capital to make informed decision of what constitutes academic success, as this requires interpretation of government educational league tables or reading of Ofsted inspection reports. This would largely be determined by the education of one or both of the parents to help make an informed choice. Thirdly, their choice may be restricted due to the size of the family, financial capability and distance they may be expected to travel. A large Muslim family surviving on one income or even government benefits may struggle to pay for bus fares for children attending a school further away. Finally, the allocation policies, catchment area of the school and type of school may also restrict families' choices.

Poverty not culture

For the outsiders they look at this area and the schools and they say that everyone that lives in this neighbourhood or send the children to the local schools have one thing in common, they are all Muslims! But the people that live in this area will tell you that poverty is perhaps the important thing we have in common.

The above example, shared by a Muslim parent in Lancashire, demonstrates how Muslim communities have more than one identity and more than one way of imagining their self-construct. Muslim identity, especially given the domestic and international attention it attracts, is an important marker of 'self' but is not the only marker. Despite this obvious statement, Muslim communities continue to be perceived through the lenses of culture and religion rather than through more pressing issues such as poverty and social class. The above observation echoes similar experiences of many affluent Arab Muslims in the United States who, prior to the events of 9/11, perceived themselves as Americans, some even perceiving themselves as 'White Americans' only to wake up after 9/11 and realise that they were Muslims (Kundnani 2014). This fixation on a cultural explanation for complex sociological problems has a long and complicated relationship especially linked to the racialisation of Muslim communities in public discourse. First, cultural pathologisation is deeply rooted in the public discourses of cultural segregation. For example, Jack Straw (2006), one-time Secretary of State under New Labour, commenting on the 'sexual grooming cases' which hit the media headlines in December 2010 following the convictions of nine men in Derby (Miah 2013a), decided to identify Pakistani culture – which is often used as a key for Muslim culture – and not as one would imagine acts of criminality, for a possible explanation. This is clear in the following Radio 4 interview following the sentencing of young men for sexually exploiting young girls.

> ...there is a specific problem which involves Pakistani heritage men...who target vulnerable young white girls. We need to get the Pakistani community to think much more clearly about why this is going on and to be more open about the problems that are leading to a number of Pakistani heritage men thinking it is OK to target white girls in this way. These young men are in a western society, in any event, they act like any other young men, they're fizzing and popping with testosterone, they want some outlet for that, but Pakistani heritage girls are off-limits and they are expected to marry a Pakistani girl from Pakistan.

Second, the cultural explanation has also helped shaped radicalisation theories, which has influenced policies on education, immigration and social policy that give precedence to culture and religion over the role of politics or foreign policy as the dominant explanation of violent extremism (Kundnani 2014). Third, the cultural paradigm absolves its citizens of any political or moral responsibility and accountability by failing to highlight some of the many challenging issues facing Muslim communities. In the following example, a young parent who had served for over five years as a governor of a Manchester secondary school with over 90 per cent Muslim pupils, reflects on her experiences of tense debates during school governors' meetings between the senior leadership team and parents over the educational underachievement of Muslim pupils, with the former using a cultural explanation and the latter focusing on wider social factors including aspects of social class.

> I stepped down as school governor after five years; every year when the GCSE results were published it was the same explanation our kids were underachieving due to cultural reasons. They used to say that our kids don't speak English as a first language or don't speak English at home or don't have a culture of learning at home. This is completely rubbish most if not all our kids were born in UK; they have a problem with speaking their mother tongue not English. Instead of taking responsibility and recognising poor children, like the working class white schools, have challenging problems the school passes the book to the local Muslim community.

Masking of social inequality

The excuse of culture given by many parents is an appropriate tool used within public discourse to acknowledge any social or structural explanations in understanding the nature of segregation within neighbourhoods or within state schools. As already noted in chapters 2 and 3, most political discourse – as articulated by key political actors since the 2001 race riots – has made little or no reference to social inequality amongst British Muslim communities. Instead, greater emphasis has been placed upon the responsibilities of minority communities to integrate or actively embrace 'British values'; this has led to further marginalisation of the Muslim community through cultural essentialising of Muslim culture.

The failure to recognise the importance of social class within the debate has led to a rather skewed public debate on integration and schooling. Unlike their middle-class Muslim colleagues, working-class Muslims do not have a romantic *weltanschauung*, or worldview, predicated upon the notion of a meritocratic society. The following observation highlights contrasting discourses on schooling from the pragmatic approach to education, as highlighted in the previous chapter. It challenges the view which all children, regardless of ethnic or socio-economic background, have an equal chance to succeed. The counter-position maintains that the educational system privileges certain groups over others in society. It argues that the meritocratic position is grounded upon a myth which only privileges certain ethnic and social classes; segregated schools are therefore a product of social inequality and can only be solved through creating a more equitable society. The only problem is that contemporary public discourse problematises ethnically segregated schools over class-based segregation, and therefore considers the former as a social threat and not the latter (Dorling 2011).

> We sent our child to the local secondary school, which happens to be all Muslims; we knew he wouldn't get to the other schools in the borough. For poor families what choice have we got? We don't have money to go into the rich areas to get a better life. It's very difficult to make ends meet – so other prioritises take over; jobs, putting food on the table and paying the bills. Working hard for some families might make a difference, but around here, you work hard to make a living.

The above observation further reinforces the socio-economic factors behind pupils attending segregated schools. It highlights the broader social factors in general and the cultural capital of parents in particular in shaping such schools. It notes how high levels of social inequality within some communities are the principal cause of ethnic segregation – in doing so it supports the view that social inequality and exclusion are the root causes of segregation. On a more poignant note, it points to the fact that ethnic school segregation is not a desired option but an unfortunate position based upon parents' current circumstances. In essence, it recognises that the key priority and objective in life for some parents isn't to get their child to the best school in the borough, but rather to ensure that basic family needs are met. This view comes through very strongly in the following observation by a young Muslim female student who, despite having the ability to pass the entrance examination of an ethnically mixed grammar school, was unable to accept the offer of admission due to her family's financial circumstances. The student further reflects upon how not only will she have to attend the local secondary school, which has a majority Muslim cohort, but missing out on the opportunity to attend the local grammar school will no doubt impact her future career prospects.

> I passed the entrance test for the local grammar school it's a mixed school and it has the best results in the North West. My parents could not afford the annual fee of £10,000 per year. That's why I had to come to this school; it has one of the worst results not in borough but in the country. What can I do, I didn't choose to come this school with 90 per cent Bangladeshi kids. If my father was middle class then my future would have been different. I think it's wrong when they try and blame us for segregation.

Muslims, segregation and double stigma

> Segregation is not a situation disadvantaged minorities have created themselves, nor have they invented the stigmas with which they are forced to live.
>
> (Merry 2011:91)

It has been made clear from the foregoing that segregated neighbourhoods and 'choice' of school are interconnected and that the relationship between the two, in the experience of parents, is largely as a result of their social class positionalities and is not based on the desire to live separate lives. In other words, the idea that segregated schools function because Muslim parents want to isolate themselves from the White communities is completely rejected.

Ethnically segregated schools, once again, in parents' experience, happen to attract poor teaching staff and, given the levels of disruptive behaviour, they also have a high staff turnover combined with low educational results which do not make them attractive educational spaces for any parents, regardless of religion or ethnic heritage.

The neighbourhoods in which these schools are located are associated with high levels of multiple deprivation, including have high crime rates, high levels of unemployment, poor health outcomes and high population density (Anderson 2010). These experiences, as noted below, not only undermine pupils' ability to nurture or maximise their full potential, but also create an environment which socially reproduces the vicious cycles of poverty and deprivation that are passed from one generation to another.

> Are you surprised that these schools do not produce any results. The school attracts all poor teachers after all who would want to come and teach in Moortown? It's the case with most schools in poor neighbourhoods. You see this area has an image problem; it's obviously going to attract all the worst teachers. I have also noticed how teachers will also come and go and won't stick around. But think about it, you have to be tough to survive these environments with problems that generational and teachers looking for jobs know which schools have a bad reputation, they won't want to put it down on their CV.

The above observation introduces the idea of 'stigma' associated with segregated schools in deprived neighbourhoods; it notes how schools in deprived neighbourhoods are usually associated with a social deficiency. The stigmas with which many of these schools are viewed have intensified following public debate on Muslim segregation. These forms of stigma are not confined to parental observations, but are also evident in Muslim pupil experiences of daily schooling. This is reinforced by the following example taken from a focus group interview of a group of female Muslim students attending a secondary state school in the north-west of England. The schools which the respondents attended were often portrayed in a negative light by the media, due to its 90 per cent Muslim cohort. They were often described as racially polarised spaces which, if unchecked, could lead to greater racial unrest within the respective communities. Further research on this topic is required, as little empirical evidence exists in regard to how the public image of a school impacts upon its pupils. The following observation provides an insight into the way in which segregated schools depicted as problematic spaces have an impact on pupil morale and self-perception. It demonstrates how the stigma of segregated schools also involves the experiences of racism in the form of both looks and gestures which signify the unwanted presence of large groups of Muslims. It further demonstrates the perception that a similar school visit made by White pupils would not attract similar racial hostility. Perhaps the important point explored within this observation is how attending segregated schools and interacting with external agencies during school trips or outings is often associated with a double stigma. The first stigma is associated with the perceived monocultural make-up of the schools while the second – and much more crucial stigma – is grounded upon their visible affiliation with Islam which is often depicted negatively in the public imagination.

> Everyone knows that we go to Westgate School because every time we go on trips only thing that people can see is 'Black face'. You know, they all stare at us because we're all Muslims. The other day we went to the Manchester BBC [British Broadcasting Cooperation] building and we got the looks.

> Yeah they all look down on us because we are from a school with people of the same colour and the same religion. I'm sure you won't get that if there were all white people turning up! They look down at us, they make us look low. I would say to myself. What is so different about me? They won't say it in your face, but you can tell in gestures and the whispers those that don't like you, you can tell.

Segregated schools as deficit

Segregated schools are often associated with high levels of social inequality and social exclusion; both of these features were seen as principal causes of segregation rather than self-segregation based upon the desire for cultural separatism. Schooling experiences by both parents and pupils were seen through the prisms of antagonism and pessimism, which they felt had an adverse effect on their future prospects of social mobility. More significantly, segregated schools further undermined their ability to nurture the relevant socio-cultural capital and neither did it provide the necessary skills to navigate complex globalised and cosmopolitan societies. The social and economic marginalisation brought about through segregation leads to a sense of powerlessness which further undermines the raw talent and skills of Muslim pupils.

Muslim parents and pupils recognised that segregated schools, predicated by their social class positionalities, have potential long-term impacts. One of the central arguments is based upon the idea that an ethnically segregated school wasn't a 'fostering nurturing and cultivating processes' (Dewey 1916:9). In light of this, some segregated schools were considered as deficit capital; it was argued that, by attending segregated state schools, young Muslims felt they were 'losing out on their educational and social experience'. In other words, Muslim pupils recognised the importance of place and the ethnic diversity of space on educational well-being and outcome, especially the impacts of these factors on social and cultural capital. In this particular case, Muslim pupils spoke against the idea of segregation by demonstrating how, largely due to their social class positioning, they were the victims of segregation. More crucially, a number of Muslim parents responded to the charge of segregation by posing the following rhetorical question: 'Why would someone in light of the recognition that ethnically segregated state schools fail through a deficit model continue to choose to attend mono-cultural schools?' This rhetorical use of language is particularly important in identifying the challenges of the normative discourse on Muslim self-segregation, by demonstrating how segregated schools have a longitudinal impact on their socio-economic future.

The *social deficit* model of segregated schools is based upon the normative consensus that Britain is a diverse multicultural society made up of diverse communities comprising not only different religious groups but also people of different identities. This is a fact, especially when one considers the 2011 UK Census which showed that in most inner London boroughs, such as Luton and Slough, and in Leicester, no one ethnic group represents the majority of the population. Moreover, over 300 languages are spoken in London, with over one million Londoners speaking a language other than English at home (Simpson 2012). Mixed schools within this perspective were seen as a microcosm of contemporary diverse society, which was seen to provide students with the relevant social skills for a multicultural life. Muslim pupils made it clear that, in light of this fact, some of those attending segregated schools were seen to be depriving themselves of the relevant knowledge, expertise and training to deal with the complexities and ambiguities arising from multiculturalism. This is clearly articulated by the following.

> I think you can learn more when you go to school with diverse people and not just your own kind. This is because if you get used to multiculturalism in school it will be easier for you when you get a job in the future

It is interesting to note how the above respondent touched upon how attending a mixed school can provide skills that will be of use for future employment opportunities. It showed how pupils recognised the importance of education as a socio-economic transition which allows students to gain relevant social experience that is crucial for future socio-economic prospects. The importance of attending a mixed school was considered to be important because it provides a space to nurture bonding and bridging forms of social capital, which are a key feature in framing segregated schools. Social capital refers to 'connections among individuals – social networks and the norms of reciprocity and trustworthiness that arise from them' (Putnam 2000:19). Putnam (2000) makes a distinction between bridging and bonding capital. Bonding capital consists of socialisation with people that are 'like you' and have the same family, religion and culture. Bridging capital occurs through interaction with people of different racial and cultural backgrounds. The importance of social capital in society is particularly relevant, especially given the decline in social capital since the 1960s that has undermined a range of traditional, social and civic practices (ibid.).

Muslim pupils felt that by attending segregated schools they were losing out on an important social process. Mixed schools, unlike segregated schools, were seen to provide advantages not only for the students but also for wider society, especially when considering how Muslim pupils have discussed the issue of segregated schools. Pupil discourses on social capital did not reflect a self-interested or narcissistic worldview, but rather projected an account of schooling that will help reflect the multicultural ideal of British society. Attending a mixed school within this context is seen either as a civic duty or participating in active citizenship; it is a way in which students felt they could contribute to a society that is multicultural. A number of respondents stressed how attending mixed schools 'was good for the society' or how mixed schools would allow pupils to develop a 'good understanding of people from different cultural and religious heritages'. The following account captures some of the concerns associated with ethnically segregated schools by demonstrating how pupils attending such schools will find it much harder to adjust to different cultural environments in the future.

> By coming to this school we have definitely lost out by not mixing with people of different backgrounds. At the end of the day when we finish school we are going to find much harder to interact. We are going to have to mix with people of different backgrounds...We don't know what they are like, it would be difficult.

The above student, who was attending a school in Oldham with a Muslim cohort of over 90 per cent, continued to provide examples of types of interaction potentially problematic in the contexts of higher education or future employment. It is important to note that the examples that were shared (as shown below) did not include aspects of general communication, based for example upon proficiency in the English language, but rather covered aspects of deeper social interactions revolving around humour and the telling of jokes. Perhaps the most revealing account focuses on how attending a mixed school may help boost levels of confidence, which is clear from the respondent's remarks on how, in a diverse environment, students may not 'open up' or may be hesitant in engaging in social dialogue.

> Yeah, we don't know how they would respond to certain statements or jokes, we don't know if they would get our jokes. Like we might say a joke and we would laugh and we would get it, but I don't know how they might react. This might lead to us not opening up because we don't know how they may respond or react or if they might find something offensive.

Conclusion

Over the past decade, politicians and public policy analysts have been concerned with understanding why Muslim communities live in segregated neighbourhoods. Attempts were also made to make sense of the visible display of ethnic clustering of certain neighbourhoods and schools in UK towns and cities. To date, explanations and policy directions have been concerned with approaching these issues through cultural determinism. This is demonstrated by the debate on Britishness and shared values as a way of tackling the issues of segregation and self-segregation, as observed in Chapter 2. Some attempts at responding to the concerns of self-segregation have been through policy measures which conflate segregation with counter-terrorism. This chapter has challenged some of those ideas associated with the premise that Muslim communities self-consciously live in encapsulated communities, and that Muslims purposefully self-segregate themselves with the intention of maintaining a parallel existence. Rather, it is clear that 'inequality producing segregation' (Merry 2011) has a major role to play in the shaping of Muslim neighbourhoods – and also the type of choice parents can make regarding the type of school their children attend. In short, ethnically segregated schools – and not self-segregation – represent the principal cause of social inequality.

It is clear that for Muslim parents and pupils attending ethnically segregated schools the question of dignity and self-respect were critical. Muslim pupils drew upon the idea of 'double stigma' or the stigmatisation of the marginalised, not only to contest the idea of self-segregation but also to convey the socio-political impacts of their experiences. They further recognised that segregation undermines the opportunities for both schooling and future career prospects by failing to provide the social and cultural capital required to escape the vicious cycle of poverty. In light of this, Muslim discourses on segregation and schooling recognised the following three crucial points regarding the question of integration (Anderson 2010). First, the building blocks for integration should not affirm a racialised discourse of culture, rather they should be seen as key features of a just society based upon equal opportunity and fairness (Rawls 1999). Second, the debate on integration should start from the democratic principles of civil, political and social rights -his is based upon the premise that segregation of social groups is the major cause of group inequality (Anderson 2010:2). Finally, integration should ultimately serve the needs of marginalised communities in society and should not affirm the changing political rhetoric of the state.

Conclusion

> Citizenship has to be understood as dynamic and revisable,
> as marked by 'conversations and re-negotiation.' A substan-
> tial conception of citizenship implies modes of dialogue that
> reconstitute the participants in significant ways. Modood
> makes clear that 'the one thing that civic inclusion does
> not consist of is an uncritical acceptance of an existing con-
> ception of citizenship, of "the rules of the game" and a
> one-sided "fitting in" of new entrants or new equals'.
>
> (Butler 2009:139)

This book has highlighted a number of fundamental issues relating to
the debate on self-segregation, Muslims and schooling. First, public
and policy discourses relating to the Muslim communities in Britain
is based upon an imaginative projection and political construction
of Muslims as the 'Other' (Said 1978). The 'Other' within public
and policy discourses draws upon standard orientalist depictions of
Muslims as irrational, untrustworthy and, above all, dishonest. The
prototypical 'Other' is then presented as antiquated, obscurantist,
culturally backward, peculiar and unchanging – Islam and Muslims
then became synonymous with violence, terrorism and religious hys-
teria. This orientalist discourse views Muslim communities through
the lens of problematized discourses and works upon the premise that
there are certain questions relating to loyalty, belonging, difference,
theology, citizenship and integration that need to be addressed.

Major socio-political and security events at an international and
domestic level have given way to policy approaches attempting to

address the *Muslim question*. The first approach views Islam as essentially anti-modern and antithetical to Western secular mores. The role of integration policies is to require Muslim communities to reject the key tenets of Islam and to assimilate into Western secular liberalism. This can be summarised as the *Islam problematic* given that attention is drawn to the religion and not to the adherents. Thus it is not surprising to note the following irony expressed by Australia's Senator Bernardi: 'Islam itself is the problem – it's not Muslims' (Harvey and Lewis 2011). The second approach sees no major conflict between Islam or Muslims and integration: the problem lies not in the 'text', but rather in the interpretation. The future of Islam and Muslims in the West lies in a liberal, depoliticised reading of the text. This can be seen as the *Muslim problematic* given that the focus of attention is placed less on the religion and more on the followers' 'practice' of segregation and extremism.

Second, the discourse of Muslim and self-segregation hesitates to include Muslims as equals and equal citizens. In light of this, equality, or even fairness are not imperatives but rather questions that are asked in relation to the Muslim question – the Trojan Horse and Muslim faith school debates demonstrate how these questions are used against Muslims. As Norton (2013:3) has recently shown, 'the liberal and democratic states of our time hesitate to extend them rights and privileges of citizenship'. Finally, the critical message emanating from the debate on the Muslim question and the values debate on integration is that both the style and substance of these discussions actively undermine the process of integration.

This book has also demonstrated a huge disconnect between the political and policy rhetoric as highlighted above and the lived realities of Muslim communities. Parental discourse on integration and choice and type of schooling has shown how integration is seen as a natural and gradual process, resulting not only from the desire to succeed but also to be *seen* to be succeeding. It is clear from the evidence presented in this book that Muslim parents reject the notion that Muslim communities develop conscious racial boundaries based upon *spatial* self-segregation with a willingness to create their own ghettos. Instead, it supports a conception of Muslim communities based on shifting geographies of ethnic settlement, signified by the shift from traditional 'segregated' Muslim neighbourhoods into more mixed and diverse areas (Finney and Simpson 2009). Parental rejection of spatial self-segregation is closely linked with attitudes to residential integration, which is inextricably linked in turn with ethnically mixed schools, with parents' desire to move into middle-class suburbia predicated on the social and economic success of their children (Finney and Simpson 2009).

More crucially, Muslim discourse on schooling and self-segregation aims to problematise normative discussion on Muslims, schooling and self-segregation by demonstrating how Muslims rupture the binary discourse of 'segregation is bad and integration is good'; this can work through the recognition that some Muslim schools in the short term may nurture segregation with a view to rewarding long-term investments of integration.

Questions relating to the unchanging Muslim 'Other' and the premise of *cultural* self-segregation also proved to be deeply problematic. The Muslim identity construct did not give precedence to the idea associated with segregation and self-segregation. Instead it showed how the attendance by Muslims of Muslim faith schools problematises contemporary debates on self-segregation. In doing so it ruptures the simplistic binary constructs of the integration-versus-segregation debate by suggesting how faith schools can provide students with the skills and ability to interact with secularism and Britishness. Muslim faith schools can be seen to be consistent with the key tenets of multiculturalism, liberal democracy and communitarian notions of citizenship. It shows, in the light of pupil experiences, that the tensions arising from the demands of the secular state and obligations of Islam are usually dealt with in a dialectical experience.

The importance of viewing the debate on integration, segregation and self-segregation through the prism of intersectionalities was also stressed. Whilst this book has argued against the idea of *self*-segregation, it does not entirely dismiss the presence of *segregation* between and within schools. First, using the culturally deterministic approach to self-segregation does not provide a robust and nuanced answer to the question of segregation *between* schools. Instead, it is clear that 'inequality producing segregation' (Merry 2001) has a major role to play in the shaping of Muslim neighbourhoods and also the type of choice parents can make regarding the type of schools their children attend. In short, ethnically segregated schools – and not self-segregation – are principally caused by social inequality. The intersectional nature of Muslim experiences of integration and seg-regation *within* schools is determined by Muslim class positionality. It is clear that ethnically mixed schools with outstanding educa-tional standards were the ideal choice for most Muslims; sadly, only Muslims with financial and cultural capital were able to exercise this choice.

The culturally deterministic approach to self-segregation further masks the internal diversity within the Muslim community, because it fails to recognise how issues of poverty and inequality play an important role in the question of Muslim agency. The dominant themes of racism and anti-Muslim prejudice, together with poverty and inequality, are key features outside the control of Muslim com-munities that not only compromise but further consolidate the experiences of segregation. The experience not only comprises the question of segregation but does so by impacting the experiences of dignity and self-respect (Taylor 1992). Group solidarity by Muslim pupils within the experience of 'sticking together' is a reaction to per-ceived and real experiences of racial harassment, which is based upon the following Khaldunian premise: 'one cannot imagine any hostile act being undertaken against anyone who has his group feeling to support him' (Ibn Khaldun 1967, vol. 1: 263). For Muslim students, this premise was fundamental to navigating through mixed school-ing, especially within a hostile environment marked by anti-Muslim prejudice following the events of 9/11 and 7/7 (Allen 2010). In light of these 'difficult periods', group solidarity plays a vital role in defend-ing 'the group' against external forces, by reinforcing and stabilising the influence of religion within the group. Pupil discourse of group solidarity revealed it to be an essentially productive and worthwhile feature of the school experience. It was clear from the pupil discourse that an affinity to fellow Muslims did not correspond to segregation – in fact, Muslim pupils rejected the idea of segregation in general and self-segregation in particular. They felt that the mixed-school experi-ence, despite its difficulties, also provided the opportunity to mix and to get to know each other. Whilst these experiences may appear to be contradictory, it was felt that group solidarity facilitated the process of mixing from a position of self-assurance.

Bibliography

Abbas, T. (2004) *The Education of British South Asians: Ethnicity, Capital and Class Structure* (New York: Palgrave).

Abbas, T. (2007) Muslim Minorities in Britain: Integration, Multiculturalism and Radicalism in the Post 7/7 Period. *Journal of Intercultural Studies.* 28 (3) 287–300.

Abdullah, U.F. (2004) *Islam the Cultural Imperative* (Illinois: Nawawi Foundation).

Afshar, H. (1989) Education: Hopes, Expectations and Achievements of Muslim Women in West Yorkshire. *Gender and Education.* 1 (3) 261–272.

Ager, A. and Strang, A. (2008) Understanding Integration: A Conceptual Framework. *Journal of Refugee Studies.* 21 (2) 166–191.

Ahmed, S. (2009) *Seen and not Heard: Voices of Young British Muslims* (Markfield: Policy Research Centre).

Ajebo, K. (2007) *Curriculum Review: Diversity & Citizenship* (London: Department Education and Skills).

Akhtar N. (2003) Pakistani Clans 'abusing' British Politics. Available at: http://news.bbc.co.uk/1/hi/magazine/3181851.stm [Accessed January 12 2008].

Alexander, C. (2000) *Asian Gangs* (London: Berg).

Alexander C. (2007) Forward. *In:* Weekes-Bernard, D. (2007) *School Choice and Ethnic Segregation: Education Decision-making among Black and Minority Parents* (London: Runnymede Trust).

Alexander, H. (2008) The Common School and the Comprehensive Ideal. *In:* Halstead, J.M. and Haydon, G. (eds) *What is Common and about Common Schools: Rational Autonomy and Moral Agency in Liberal Education* (Oxford: Wiley Blackwell).

Ali, A. (2010) Assimilation, Integration or *Convivencia*: The Dilemma of Diaspora Muslims from 'Eurabia' to 'Londonstan', from Lakembanon to Sri Lanka. *Journal of Muslim Minority Affairs.* 30 (2) 183–198.

Al-Alwani, T.J. (2003) *Towards a Fiqh for Minorities.Surrey* (London: IIIT).

Allen, C. (2010) *Islamophobia* (London: Ashgate).

Allen, K. (2014) Welfare Cuts Drive UK's Poorest Families Deeper into Poverty, says Oxfam. Available at: http://www.theguardian.com/politics/2014/apr/22/welfare-cuts-drive-uk-poorest-poverty-oxfam [Accessed 13th June 2014].

Almond, B. (1994) In Defence of Choice in Education. *In:* Halstead, J.M. (ed.) (1994) *Parental Choice and Education: Principles, Policy and Practice* (London: Kogan Page).

Alport, G.W. (1979) *The Nature of Prejudice* (Cambridge: Cambridge University Press).

Alvi, A. (2010) The Hijab: 20 Years On? Available at: http://www.the-platform.org.uk/2010/02/14/the-hijaab-20-years-on/ [Accessed 16 March 2013].

Ammann, D. (2009) The Real Reasons Why the Swiss Voted to Ban Minarets. Available at: http://www.huffingtonpost.com/daniel-ammann/the-real-reasons-why-the_b_373947.html [Accessed 1 January 2014].

Anderson, B. (1983) *Imagined Communities: Reflections on the Origin and Spread of Nationalism* (London: Verso).

Anderson, E. (2010) *The Imperative of Integration* (Princeton: Princeton University Press).

Ansari, H. (2004) *The Infidel Within: The Muslim History of Britain 1800 to the Present* (London: Hurst).

Apple, M. and Buras, K. (eds) (2006) *The Subaltern Speak: Curriculum, Power and Educational Struggles* (London: Routledge).

Archer, L. (2003) *Race, Masculinity and Schooling: Muslim Boys and Education* (Maindenhead: Open University Press).

Archer, L. (2011) Constructing Minority Ethnic Middle-Class Identity: An Exploratory Study with Parents, Pupils and Young Professionals. *Sociology*. 45 (1) 134–152.

Arkoun, M. (1994) *Rethinking Islam: Common Questions, Uncommon Answers* (Boulder: Westview Press).

Auda, J. (2008) *Maqasid al-Shariah* (Washington, DC: IIIT).

Bains, I. and Spencer, B. (2013) Female Teachers at Islamic School 'Made to Sign Contract Agreeing to Wear Headscarf Even if They're NOT Muslim'. Available at: http://www.dailymail.co.uk/news/article-2426626/Female-teachers-Islamic-school-sign-contract-agreeing-wear-headscarf-theyre-NOT-Muslim.html. [Accessed 14 June 2014].

Baker, M. (1981) *New Racisms: Conservatives and the Ideology of the Tribes* (London: Junction Books).

Ball, S. (2013) *Foucault, Power and Education* (London: Routledge).

Banton, M. (1967) *Race Relations* (London: Tavistock).

Banton, M. (2001) National Integration in France and Britain. *Journal of Ethnic and Migration Studies*. 27(1) 151–168.

Barnard, H and Turner, C. (2011) *Poverty and Ethnicity: A Review of Evidence* (York: Joseph Rowntree Foundation).

Barry, B. (2001) *Culture Equality* (Cambridge: Polity).

Basit, T. (1997) 'I Want More Freedom, but Not Too Much': British Muslim Girls and Dynamism of Family Values. *Gender and Education*. 9 (4) 425–439.

Bauman, Z. (1991) *Modernity and Ambivalence* (New York: Ithaca).

Bauman, Z. (2000) *Liquid Modernity* (Oxford: Polity Press).

Bauman, Z. and Testler, K. (2001) *Conversations with Zygmunt Bauman* (Cambridge: Polity).

Beck, L., Keith, M., Khan, A., Shukra, K. and Solomas, J. (2002) The Return of Assimilation: Race and Multiculturalism and New Labour. *Sociological Research Online*, 7 (2): Available at: http://www.socresonline.org.uk/7/2/back.html [Accessed 17 July 2007].

Begg, M. (2006) *Enemy Combatant* (London: Free Press).

Begg, M. (2008) Moazam Begg in Conversation with Gareth Pearce. Available at: http://cage.b786-3-staging.co.uk/article/moazzam-begg-conversation-gareth-peirce [Accessed 20 March 2013].

Bell, D. (2004) *Silent Covenants* (Oxford: Oxford University Press).

Bew, J. and Mayer, S. (2014) Blowback: Who are Isis and Why are Young Brits Fighting with Them? *The New Statesman,* 23 June 2014.

Bhabha, H.K. (1994) *The Location of Culture* (London: Routledge).

Bhatcharyya, G. (2008) *Dangerous Brown Men* (London: Zed Books).

Birt, Y. (2009) Promoting Virulent Envy? Reconsidering the UK's Terrorist Prevention Strategy. *RUSI.* 154 (4) 52–58.

Blair, T. (2006) Our Nation's Future – Multiculturalism and Integration. Available at: http://www.number10.gov.uk/output/Page10563.asp [Accessed 14th July 2009].

Blond, P. (2010) *Red Tory* (London: Faber and Faber).

Boeijie, H. (2010) *Analysis in Qualitative Research* (London: Sage).

Bonnet, A. (2000) *White Identities: Historical and International Perspectives* (Essex: Prentice Hall).

Bourdieu, P. (1986) The Forms of Capital. *In*: Richardson, J.E. (ed.) *The Handbook of Theory of Research for the Sociology of Education* (London: Greenwood Press).

Bourdieu, P. and Passerson, J.K. (1999) *Reproduction in Education, Society and Culture* (London: Sage).

Bowen, J.R. (2007) *Why the French Don't Like the Headscarf?* (Princeton: Princeton University Press).

Bowskill, M., Lyons, E. and Coyle, A. (2007) The Rhetoric of Acculturation: When Integration Means Assimilation. *British Journal of Social Psychology.* 46 793–813.

Brittain, V. (2008) Besieged in Britain. *Race and Class.* 50 (3) 1–30.

Brown, G. (2006) The Future of Britishness. Available at: http://www.fabians.org.uk/events/speeches/the-future-of-britishness [Accessed 16 December 2009].

Brown, P. (1994) Education and Ideology of Parentocracy. *In*: Halstead, J.M. (ed.) (1994) *Parental Choice and Education: Principles, Policy and Practice* (London: Kogan Page).

Burdsey, D. (2007) Role with the Punches: The Construction and Representation of Amir Khan as a Role Model for Multiethnic Britain. *The Sociological Review.* 55 (3) 611–631.

Burchell, G., Gordon, C., and Miller, P. (1991) *The Foucault Effect: Studies in Governmentality* (Chicago: Chicago University Press).

Burgess, S. and Wilson, D. (2004) School Segregation in Multiethnic England. *Ethnicities.* 4 (2) 237–265.

Burgess, S. and Wilson, D. and Richard, H. (2006) *School and Residential Ethnic Segregation: An Analysis of Variations across England's Local Education Authorities.* CMPO Working Paper Series No. 06/145.

Butler, J. (2004) *Precarious Life: The Powers of Mourning and Violence* (London: Verso).

Butler, J. (2009) *Frames of War: When is Life Grievable?* (London: Seagul Books).

Butler, P. (2014) Hunger is a 'National Crisis', Religious Leaders Tell Cameron. Available at: http://www.theguardian.com/society/2014/apr/16/ million-people-britain-food-banks-religious-leaders-faith-groups [Accessed 13 June 2014].

Caldwell, C. (2009) *Reflections on the Revolution in Europe: Immigration, Islam, and the West* (London: Allen Lane).

Cameron, D. (2011a) PM's Speech at Munich Security Conference. 5 February. Available at: http://number10.gov.uk/speeches-and-transcripts/ 2011/02/pms-speech [Accessed 14 April 2011].

Cameron, D. (2011b) Commemorating the Version's 400th Anniversary. 16 December 2011. Available at: https://www.gov.uk/government/news/ prime-ministers-king-james-bible-speech [Accessed 30 July 2014].

Cantle, T. (2001) *Community Cohesion: A Report of the Independent Review Team* (London: Home Office).

Cantle, T. (2005) *Community Cohesion: A New Framework for Race and Diversity* (Basingstoke: Palgrave Macmillan).

Cantle, T. (2012) *Interculturalism: The New era of Cohesion and Diversity* (Basingstoke: Palgrave Macmillan).

Cary, Lord. (2008) Are we Promoting Harmony or Muslim Ghettos? *Daily Telegraph*, 09 February.

Cashin, S. (2004) *The Failure of Integration: How Race and Class are Undermining the American Dream* (New York: Public Affairs).

Cessari, J. (2004) *When Islam and Democracy Meet: Muslims in Europe and in the United States* (Basingstoke: Palgrave).

Clarke, T. (2001) *Burnley Task Force Report on the Disturbances in June2001* (Burnley: Burnley Borough Council).

Cockburn, P. (2015) *The Rise of Islamic State: ISIS and the New Sunni Revolution.* (London :Verso).

Cohen, E.G. (1980) *Design and Re-Design of the De-Segregated School: Problems of State Power and Conflict* (New York: State University).

Cohen, S. (2011) *Folk Devils and Moral Panic* (London: Routledge).

Cole, M.I. (2008) *Every Muslim Child Matters. Practical Guidance for Schools and Children Services* (Stoke on Trent: Trentham).

Collins, R. (1986) *Max Weber* (London: Sage).

Crick, B. (1998) *Education for Citizenship and the Teaching of Democracy in Schools* (London: Qualification and Curriculum Authority).

Crozier, G. and Davies, J. (2008) 'The Trouble is they Don't Mix': Self Segregation or Enforced Exclusion? *Race, Ethnicity and Education.* 11 (3) 285–301.

Cumper, P. (1994) Racism, Parental Choice and the Law. *In*: Halstead, J.M. (ed.) (1994) *Parental Choice and Education: Principles, Policy and Practice* (London: Kogan Page).

Curtis, P. (2009) Academies: 200 and Counting, but more Doubts Raised. *Guardian*, 07 September.

Daily Mail (2008) Muslim Faith Schools Cause Segregation. *Daily Mail*, 29 July.

Daniel, N. (1991) *Islam and the West: The Making of an Image* (London: Oneworld).

Darlymple, T. (2002) The Man who Predicted the Riots. *City Journal.* Spring 2002. Available at: http://www.city-journal.org/html/12_2_oh_to_be.html [Accessed on May 2007].

Davies, L. (2008) *Educating Against Extremism* (Stoke on Trent: Trentham Books).

Delgado, R. (ed.) (1995) *Critical Race Theory: The Cutting Edge* (Philadelphia: Temple University Press).

Dench, G., Gavron, K. and Young, M. (2006) The *New East End: Kinship, Race and Conflict* (London: Profile Books).

Department of Children, Schools and Families (DCSF) (2007) *Guidance on the Duty to Promote Community Cohesion* (London: The Stationery Office).

Department of Children, Schools and Families (DCSF) (2008) *Learning Together to Be Safe: A Toolkit to Help Schools Contribute to the Prevention of Violent Extremism* (London: The Stationery Office).

Department of Education (2010) *Evaluation of the Schools Linking Network: Final Report* (London: The Stationery Office).

Department of Education (2013) Lord Nash Letter to the Chair of the Al-Madinah Education Trust. Available at: https://www.gov.uk/government/publications/lord-nash-letter-to-the-chair-of-the-al-madinah-education-trust–2 [Accessed 6 July 2014].

Department of Education (2014) Lord Nash Letter to Al-Madinah Education Trust. Available at: https://www.gov.uk/government/publications/letter-from-lord-nash-to-al-madinah-education-trust [Accessed 6 July 2014].

Dewey, J. (1916) *Democracy and Education* (New York: Free Press).

Diwan, K. (2008) *Education for Inclusive Citizenship* (London: Routledge).

Dixon, J., Durkeim, K. and Tredaux, C. (2005) Beyond the Optimal Contact Strategy. A Reality Check for the Contact Hypothesis. *American Psychologist.* 60 697–711.

Djait, H. (1985) *Europe and Islam* (Berkeley: University of California Press).

Dodd, V. (2009) Government Anti-terrorism Strategy 'Spies' on Innocent. *The Guardian*, 17 October.

Dorling, D. (2011) *Injustice: Why Social Inequality Persists* (Portland: Polity Press).

DuBois, W.E.B. (1999) *The Souls of Black Folk* (Oxford: Oxford University Press).

Durkhiem, E. (1984) *The Divisions of Labour in Society* (London: Free Press).

Eade, J. (1989) *The Politics of Community: The Bangladeshi Community in East London* (Aldershot: Avebury).

East London Mosque (2013) *Unwelcome 'Patrols'.* Available at: http://archive.eastlondonmosque.org.uk/news/390 [Accessed 3 April 2014].

Elgot, J. (2014) 'Christian Patrols' Warning in East London Investigated by Police. *The Huffington Post.* Available at: http://www.huffingtonpost.co.uk/2014/02/05/christian-patrols-tower-h_n_4729611.html [Accessed 20 July 2014].

El-Affendi, A.A. (2009) The People on the Edge: Religious Reform and the Burden of the Western Muslim Intellectual. *Harvard Middle Eastern and Islamic Review*, 8 19–50.

Erick, C. (2010) *Race-Class Relations and Integration in Secondary Education: The Case of Miller High* (New York: Palgrave).

Sioni, A. (1993) *The Spirit of Community: The Reinvention of American Society* (London: Touchstone Books).

Fanon, F. (1967) *Black Skin White Mask* (New York: Grove Press).

Fekete, L. (2008) *Integration, Islamaphobia and Civil Rights in Europe* (London: Institute for Race Relations).

Fekete, L. (2009) *A Suitable Enemy Racism, Migration and Islamophobia* (London: Pluto Books).

Felzer, J.S. and Soper, C.J. (2005) *Muslims and the State in Britain, France, and Germany* (Cambridge: Cambridge University Press).

Ficher, C.S. (2001) *Bowling Alone: What's the Score?* Paper Presented at 'Author Meets Critic: Putnam, *Bowling Alone*' Session of the Meetings of the American Sociological Association, Anaheim, California, August 2001. Available at: [http://ucdata.berkeley.edu/rsfcensus/papers/BowlingAlone.pdf] [Accessed 4 July 2011].

Finney, N. and Simpson, L. (2009) *Sleepwalking To Segregation'? Challenging Myths about Race And Migration* (Bristol: Policy Press).

Flint, J. and Robinson, D. (eds) (2008) *Community Cohesion in Crisis? New Dimensions of Diversity and Difference* (Bristol: Policy Press).

Forrest, A. (2014) Muslim Groups are Putting their Faith in Food Banks to Help Tackle Poverty. *The Guardian*, 2 April 2014.

Foucault, M. (1969) *The Archaeology of Knowledge* (London: Tavistock).

Gadher, D. (2013) 'Shariah Patrols Snatch Drinks from Passers-by'. *Sunday Times*, 20 January.

Gammell, C. (2008) Britain's Youngest Teenage Terrorist: 'A Wake-up Call for Parents'. *Daily Telegraph*, 19 September.

Garner, R. (2007) Multi-Faith School Planned to Tackle Segregation. *The Independent*, 6 February.

Gergan, K.J. (1985) 'Social Constructionist Approach': Context and Implication. *In*: Gergan, K.J. and Davies, K. (1985) *The Social Construction of the Person* (New York: Springer-Verlag).

Gilborn, D. (1995) *Racism and Anti-Racism in Real Schools* (Buckingham: Open University Press).

Gilborn, D. (2008) *Racism and Education: Coincidence or Conspiracy* (London: Routledge).

Gilligan, A. (2010) Ofsted praises Islamic schools which oppose Western lifestyle. *The Telegraph*, 6 November. Available at: http://www.telegraph.co.uk/education/educationnews/8114452/Ofsted-praises-Islamic-schools-which-oppose-Western-lifestyle.html [Accessed January 2013].

Gilroy, P. (1987) *There Ain't No Black In the Union Jack: The Cultural Politics of Race and Nation* (London: Hutchinson).

Gilroy, P. (1993) *The Black Atlantic: Modernity and Double Consciousness* (London: Verso).

Glazer, N. (1997) *We are All Multiculturalists Now* (Cambridge: Cambridge University Press).

Goldberg, D.T. (2002) *The Racial State* (London: Blackwell).

Goldthorpe, J.H., Lockwood, D., Bechhofer, F. and Platt, J. (1963) *The Affluent Worker: Political Attitudes and Behaviour* (Cambridge: Cambridge University Press).

Goodhart, D. (2004) Discomfort of Strangers, *The Guardian*, 24 February.

Goodwin, M.J. (2011) *New British fascism: rise of the British National Party (BNP)* (London: Routledge).

Gordon, M.M. (1964) *Assimilation in American Life* (Oxford: Oxford University Press).

Green, N. (2006) Time and the Study of Assimilation. *Rethinking History*. 10 (2) 239–258.

Grillo, R.D. (1998) *Pluralism and the Politics of Difference: State, Culture and Ethnicity in Comparative Perspective* (Oxford: Clarendon Press).

Guha, R. (1982) On Some Aspects of the Historiography of Colonial India. *In*: Guha, R. (1982) (ed.) *Subaltern Studies 1: Writings on South Asian History and Society* (New Delhi: Oxford India Paperbacks).

Hall, M. (2009) Muslim Schools to Ban our Culture. *Daily Express*, 20 February.

Hall, S. (1973) *Encoding and Decoding in the Television Discourse* (Birmingham: Centre for Contemporary Cultural Studies).

Hall, S. (1992) New Ethnicities. *In*: Donald, J. and Ali, R. (eds) *'Race' Culture and Difference* (London: Open University Press).

Hall, S., Critcher, C., Jefferson, T., Clarke, J. and Roberts, B. (1978) *Policing the Crisis* (London: Macmillan).

Halstead, J.M. (1986) *The Case for Muslim Voluntary Aided Schools: Some Philosophical Reflections* (Cambridge: Islamic Academy).

Halstead, J.M. (1988) *Education, Justice and Diversity; An Examination of the Honeyford Affair 1984–1985* (London: Falmer).

Halstead, J.M. (1991) Radical Feminism, Islam and the Single Sex Debate. *Gender and Education*. 3 (3) 263–278.

Halstead, J.M. (ed.) (1994a) *Parental Choice and Education: Principles, Policy and Practice* (London: Kogan Page).

Halstead, J.M. (1994b) Parental Choice: An Overview. *In*: Halstead, J.M. (ed.) *Parental Choice and Education: Principles, Policy and Practice* (London: Kogan Page).

Halstead, J.M. (1996a) 'Values and Values: Education: Education in Schools'. *In*: Halstead, M.J. and Taylor, M.J. (eds) *Values in Education and Education in Values* (London: Falmer).

Halstead, J.M. (1996b) Liberal Values and Liberal Education. *In*: Halstead, M.J. and Taylor, M.J. (eds) *Values in Education and Education in Values* (London: Falmer).

Halstead, J.M. (2005) Islam, Homophobia and Education: A Reply to Michael Merry. *Journal of Moral Education*. 34 (1) 37–42.

Halstead, J.M. (2008) In Place of a Conclusion: The Common School and the Melting Pot. *In*: Halstead, J.M. and Haydon, G. (eds) *The Common School and the Comprehensive Ideal* (London: Wiley Blackwell).

Halstead, J.M. (2009) In Defence of Faith Schools. *In*: Haydon, G. (ed.) *Faith in Education: A Tribute to Terence McLaughlin* (London: Institute of Education).

Halstead, J.M. and McLaughlin, T. (2005a) Are Faith Schools Divisive? *In*: Cairns, J., Gardner, R. and Lawton, D. (eds) *Faith Schools: Consensus or Conflict?* (London: Routledge).

Halstead, J.M. and Taylor, M.J. (1996) *Values in Education and Education in Values* (London: Falmer).

Harvey, D. (1996) *Justice, Nature and the Geography of Difference* (Oxford: Blackwell).

Harvey, M. and Lewis, S. (2011) Islam's the Problems, not Muslims, says Senator Cory Bernardi. *Herald Sun*, 19 February [Online] Available at: http://www.news.com.au/national/islams-the-problems-not-muslims-says-senator-cory-bernardi/story-e6frfkvr-1226008540417#ixzz1g9oDZskx [Accessed 15 September 2011].

Haw, K.F. (1994) Muslim Girls' School – A Conflict of Interest? *Gender and Education*. 6 (1) 63–76.

Haydon, G. (2008) In Search of the Comprehensive Ideal. *In*: Halstead, J.M. and Haydon, G. (eds) (2008) *The Common School and the Comprehensive Ideal* (London: Wiley Blackwell).

Haydon, G. (ed.) (2009) *Faith in Education: A Tribute to Terence McLaughlin* (London: Institute of Education).

Henry, J. (2008) City Academies Spell Good News for Education. *Telegraph*, 16 August 2008.

Hesse, B. (ed.) (2000) *Un/Settled Multiculturalism: Diasporas, Entanglement, Transruptions* (London: Zed Books).

Hewer, C. (2001) Muslim Schools. *Oxford Review of Education*. 27 (4) 515–527.

Hewitt, R. (2005) *White Backlash and the Politics of Multiculturalism* (Cambridge: Cambridge University Press).

Hewstone, M. (2006) *Living Apart, Living Together? The Role of Inter-group Contact in Social Integration* (Joint British Academy/British Psychological Society Lecture).

Hewstone, M. and Brown, R. (1986) *Contact & Conflict in Inter-group Encounters* (London: Blackwell).

Hewstone, M., Paolini, S., Cairns, E., Voci, A. and Harwood, J. (2006) Intergroup Contact and the Promotion of Intergroup Harmony. *In*: Brown R.J. and Capozza, D (eds) (2006) *Social Identities: Motivational, Emotional, Cultural Influences* (Hove: Psychology Press).

Hewstone, M., Tausch, N., Hughes, J. and Cairns, E. (2007) Prejudice, Intergroup Contact and Identity: Do Neighbourhoods Matter. *In*: Wetherall, M., Lafleche, M. and Berkley, R. (eds) (2007) *Identity, Ethnic Difference and Community Cohesion* (London: Sage).

Holehouse, M. (2014) Cabinet Reshuffle: David Cameron 'Will Pledge to Pull Britain out of European Right Body'. Available at: http://www.telegraph.co.uk/news/politics/10969806/Cabinet-reshuffle-David-Cameron-will-pledge-to-pull-Britain-out-of-European-right-body.html [Accessed 21 July 2014].

Home Office (2002) *Safe Borders, Safe Haven: Integration with Diversity in Modern Britain* (London: Stationery Office).

Honeyford, R. (1983a) Multi-ethnic Intolerance. *The Salisbury Review*, Summer.

Honeyford, R. (1983b) When East is West. *Times Educational Supplement*, 2 September.

Honeyford, R. (1984) Education and Race-an Alternative View. *The Salisbury Review*, Winter, pp. 30–32.

Honeyford, R. (1985) The right education? *The Salisbury Review*, January, pp. 28–30.

Honeyford, R. (1988) *Integration or Disintegration?* (London: Calridge).

Honeyford, R. (2006) Education and Race: An Alternative View. *Daily Telegraph*, 27 August.

HM Government (2006) *Countering International Terrorism: The United Kingdom's Strategy*, Cm 6888, (London: The Stationary Office).

HM Government (2009) *The United Kingdom's Strategy for Countering International Terrorism*. (London: Home Office).

HM Government (2011) Prevent Strategy, Cm 8092, (London: The Stationary Office).

House of Commons, Home Affairs Select Committee (2005) *Terrorism and Community Relations, Sixth Report of Sessions 2004–2005*, Volume 1 [Report Together with Formal Minutes and Appendix]. HC 165–1, London: The Stationary Office.

House of Commons (2010) Communities and Local Government Committee, *Preventing Violent Extremism, Sixth Report of Sessions 2009–10*, HC 65, (London: The Stationary Office).House of Commons (Public Accounts Committee) (2008–2009) *Building Schools for the Future: Renewing the Secondary School Estate*. Twenty-Seventh Report of Session (London: The Stationery Office).

House of Commons (Education Commitee) (2014) *Extremism in schools* [Online] Available at: http://www.parliamentlive.tv/Main/Player.aspx?meetingId=15743 [Accessed on 20 August 2014].

Hussain, S. (2008) *Muslims on the Map: A National Survey of Social Trends in Britain*. International Library of Human Geography (IB Tauris: London).

Hutchinson, A. and Rosser, I. (2005) Class Warfare. *Yorkshire Evening Post*, 8 September.

Ibn Khaldun [Ibn Khaldun, 'Abd al-Rahman] (1967) *Ibn Khaldun: The Muqadimmah – An Introduction to History* (3 vols), trans. Franz Rosenthal (London: Routledge and Kegan Paul).

Ibn Khadun [Ibn Khaldun, 'Abd al-Rahman] (2005) *Ibn Khaldun: The Muqadimmah – An Introduction to History*, trans. Franz Rosenthal, abridged and edited by N.J. Daood (Princeton: Princeton University Press).

Imtiaz, A.S. (2010) *Wandering Lonely in a Crowd: Reflections on the Muslim Condition in the West* (Markfield: Kube Press).

Jacoby, W. and Yavuz, H. (2008) Modernization, Identity and Integration: An Introduction to Special Issue on Islam and Europe. *Journal of Muslim Minority Affairs*. 28 (1) 1–6.

Jay, T. (2005) Integration: Could Islamic Schools be part of the solution? *News and World Report*. 139 (19) 37–40.

Jenkins, R. (1967) *Essays and Speeches* (New York: Chilmark).

Johnston, R., Burgess, S., Wilson, D. and Harris, R. (2006) School and Residential Ethnic Segregation: An Analysis of Variations across England's Local Education Authorities. *Regional Studies*. 40 (9) 973–990.

Johnston, R., Poulsen, M. and Forrest, J. (2004) On Measurement and Meaning of Residential Segregation: A Response to Simpson. *Urban Studies*. 42 (7) 1221–1227.

Joppke, C. (2009) Limits of Integration Policy: British and Her Muslim. *Journal of Ethnic and Migration Studies*. 35 (3) 453–472.

Joppke, C. and Morawska, E. (2003) *Toward Assimilation and Citizenship: Immigrants in Liberal Nation-States* (New York: Palgrave).

Kalra, V.S. (2002) Extended View: Riots, Race and Reports: Denham, Cantle, Oldham and Burnley Inquiries. *SAGE Race Relations Abstracts*. 27 (4) 21–30.

Kalra, V., Kaur, R. and Hutnyk, J. (2005) *Diaspora and Hybridity* (London: Sage).

Kalra, V.S. and Kapoor, N. (2008) *Interrogating Segregation, Integration and the Community Cohesion Agenda*. CCSR Working Paper 2008–16. Cathie Marsh Centre for Census and Survey Research. Available at: http://www.ccsr.ac.uk/publications/working/ [Accessed December 2008].

Khaleel, H. (2012) The Curry Crisis. *The Guardian*, 8 January. Available at: http://www.theguardian.com/lifeandstyle/2012/jan/08/britains-curry-crisis-chefs-immigration [Accessed June 2013].

Kintre, K., Bannister, J., Pickerin, J., Reid, M. and Suzuki, N. (2008) *Young People and Territoriality in British Cities* (York: Joseph Rowntree Foundation).

Kudenko, I.D.P. (2009) The Model of Integration? Social and Spatial Transformation in the Leeds Jewish Community. *Journal of Ethnic and Migration Studies*. 35 (9) 1533–1549.

Kundanani, A. (2007) *The End of Tolerance: Racism in 21st Century Britain* (London: Pluto Press).

Kundanani, A. (2009) *Spooked! How Not To Prevent Violent Extremism* (London: Institute of Race Relations).

Kundanani, A. (2014) *The Muslims are Coming!* (London: Verso).

Kymlicka, W. (1989) *Multicultural Citizenship* (Oxford: Clarendon Press).

Laborde, C. (2008) *Critical Republicanism* (Oxford: Oxford University Press).

Lareau, A. (2003) *Unequal Childhoods: Class, Race, and Family Life* (Berkeley: University of California).

Lawrence, J. and Vaise, J. (2006) *Integrating Islam: Political and Religious Challenges in Contemporary France* (Washington: Brookings Institute).

Leicester, M. (1989) *Multicultural Education: From Theory to Practice* (Windsor: NFER/Nelson).

Levin, S., Van Larr, C. and Sidanius, J. (2003) The Effects of in Group and Out Group Friendship on Ethnic Attitudes in College: A Longitudinal Study. *Group Process and Intergroup Relations*. 6 76–92.

Levinson, M. (2008) School and the Comprehensive Ideal. *In*: Halstead, J.M. and Haydon, G. (eds) *The Common School and the Comprehensive Ideal* (London: Wiley Blackwell).

Lymperopoulou, K. and Parameshwaran, M. (2014) How are Ethnic Inequalities in Education Changing? Joseph Rowntree Foundation & University of Manchester. ESRC Centre on Dynamics of Ethnicity (Code).

MacDonald, I. (1989) *Murder in the Playground* (London: Longsight Press).

MacEoin, D. (2009) *Music, Chess and Other Sins* (London: Civitas).

Mac an Ghaill, M. (2010) Educating for Political Activity: A Younger Generational Response. *Educational Review*, 62 (4):1–12.

Mac an Ghaill, M. (1999) *Contemporary Racisms and Ethnicities: Social and Cultural Transformations* (Buckingham: Open University Press).

Mac an Ghaill, M. (1994) *The Making of Men: Schooling, Masculinities and Sexualities* (Buckingham:Open University Press).

Mac an Ghaill, M. (1992) *Young, Gifted and Black: The Schooling of Black Youth* (Buckingham: Open University Press).

March, A.F. (2009a) *Islam and Liberal Citizenship: The Search for an Overlapping Consensus* (Oxford: Oxford: University Press).

March, A.F. (2009b) Sources of Moral Obligation to non-Muslims in the 'Jurisprudence of Muslim Minorities' (Fiqh al-aqalliyyat) Discourse. *Islamic Law and Society*. 16 (1) 34–94.

Malik, M. (2009) Anti-Muslim Prejudice in the West, Past and Present: An Introduction. *Patterns of Prejudice*. 43 (3/4) 207–212.

Marranci, G. (2004) Multiculturalism, Islam, and the Clash of Civilization Theory: Rethinking Islamophobia. *Culture and Religion*. 5 (1) 107–119.

Marshall (1950) *Citizenship and Social Class* (Cambridge: Cambridge University Press).

Massey, D.S. and Denton, N.A. (1988) The Dimensions of Residential Segregation. *Social Forces*. 67 281–315.

McCreary, E., Jones, L. and Holmes, R. (2007) Why do Muslim Parents Want Muslim Schools? *Journal of International Research and Development*. 27 (3) 203–219.

McGee, D. (2003) Moving to 'Our' Common Ground – A Critical Examination of Community Cohesion Discourse in Twenty First Century Britain. *Sociological Review*. 51 (3) 376–404.

McGee, D. (2008) *The End of Multiculturalism: Terrorism, Integration and Human Rights* (Berkshire: Open University Press).

McLaughlin, T. (1992) The Ethics of Separate Schools. *In*: Leicester, M. and Taylor, M. (eds) (1992) *Ethics, Ethnicity and Education* (London: Kogan Page).

McNally, T. (2010) European Convention on Human Rights is part of Britain's DNA. *The Guardian*, 21 November. Available at: http://www.theguardian.com/commentisfree/libertycentral/2010/nov/21/convention-human-rights-britain-coalition [Accessed 20 July 2014].

Meer, N. (2007) Muslim Schools in Britain: Challenging Mobilisations or Logical Developments. *Asia Pacific Journal of Education*. 27 (1) 55–71.

Meer, N. (2010) *Citizenship, Identity and the Politics of Multiculturalism: The Rise of Muslim Consciousness* (London: Palgrave).

Meer, N. and Modood, T. (2010) Racialisation of Muslims. *In*: Sayyid, S. and Vakil, A. (eds) (2010) *Thinking Through Islamophobia* (London: Hurst).

Meer, N. and Modood, T. (2012) How does Interculturalism Contrast with Multiculturalism?. *Journal of Intercultural Studies*. 33 (2), 175–196.

Meer, N. (2013) Race, Culture and Difference in the Study of Antisemitism and Islamophobia. *Ethnic and Racial Studies*. 36 (3), 385–398.

Meer, N. & Modood, T. (2014) Cosmopolitanism and integrationism: Is multiculturalism in Britain a zombie category?,*Identities: Global Studies in Culture and Power*. 21 (6), 658–674.

Merry, M.S. (2005) Should Educators Tolerate Intolerance? Mark Halstead, Homosexuality and the Islamic Case. *Journal of Moral Education*. 34 (1) 19–36.

Merry, M.S. (2012) Equality, Self-respect and Voluntary Separation. *Critical Review of International Social and Political Philosophy*. 15 (1) 79–100.

Merry, M.S. (2013) *Equality, Citizenship and Segregation: A Defense of Separation* (New York: Palgrave Macmillan).

Metcalf, B. (2002) *Islamic Revival in British India: Deoband, 1860–1900* (New Delhi: Oxford University Press).

Miah, S. (2012) School de-segregation and the Politics of 'Forced Integration'. *Race and Class*. 54 (2) 26–39.

Miah, S. (2013a) 'Prevent'ing Education: Anti-Muslim Racism and the War on Terror in Schools. *In*: Kapoor, N., Kalra, V. and Rhodes, J. (eds). *The State of Race* (Basingstoke: Palgrave).

Miah, S. (2013b) Muslim Group Solidarity and Schooling. *In*: Alexander, C., Redclift, V. and Hussain, A. (eds). *The New Muslims* (London: Runnymede Trust).

Miah, S. (2014) Trojan Horse, Ofsted and the 'Prevent'ing of Education. *Discover Society*. Available at: http://www.discoversociety.org/2014/07/01/trojan-horse-ofsted-and-the-preventing-of-education/ [Accessed 15 July 2014].

Miller, K., Kite, M., Orr, J., Goswami, N. and Nikkhah, R. (2008) Head Teacher who Never Taught Again after Daring to Criticise Multiculturalism, *Daily Telegraph*, 22 August.

Millner, R. H. (2007) Race Culture and Researcher Positionality: Working Through Dangers Seen, Unseen and Unforseen. *Educational Researcher*. 36 (7), pp. 388–400.

Modood, T. (2005) *Multicultural Politics: Racism, Ethnicity and Muslims in Britain* (Edinburgh : Edinburgh University Press).

Modood, T. (2007) *Multiculturalism: A Civic Idea* (Cambridge: Polity).

Modood, T. (2010) *Still Not Easy Being British: Struggles for Multicultural Citizenship*. (Stoke on Trent: Trentham Books).

Modood, T. and Triandafyllidon Zapaton-Borrero, R. (2006) *Multiculturalism, Muslims and Citizenship: European Approach* (London: Routledge).

Mogahed, D. (2009) *The Gallup Coexist Index 2009: A Global Study of Interfaith Relation* (New York: The Coexist Foundation).

Mogahed, D. and Nyri, Z. (2007) Reinventing Integration. *Harvard International Review*. August 2007.

Mullard, C. (1982) Multiracial Education in Britain: From Assimilation to Cultural Pluralism. *In*: Tiernay, J (ed.) *Race, Migration and Schooling* (London: Holt).

Murphy, P. (2008) Pupils have had Enough of Being Guinea Pigs. *Yorkshire Evening Post*, 9 October 2008.

Naylor, F. (1989) *Dewsbury: The School above the Pub: A Case Study in Multicultural Education* (London: Educational Research Trust).

Nazir-Ali, M. (2008) Extremism Flourished as UK lost Christianity. *Daily Telegraph*, 6 January.

Odone, C. (2008) *In Bad Faith: The New Betrayal in Faith Schools* (London: Centre for Policy Studies).

Office for Standards in Education (Ofsted) (2012) The Framework for School Inspection. Available at: http://www.ofsted.gov.uk/resources/framework-for-school-inspection-september-2012-0 [Accessed August 2012].

Office for Standards in Education (Ofsted) (2014) The Framework for School Inspection. Available at: https://www.gov.uk/government/publications/the-framework-for-school-inspection [Accessed June 2014].

Office for Standards in Education (Ofsted) (2013) Al Madinah School: School Inspection Report. Available at: www.ofsted.gov.uk/filedownloading/?id=2276225&type= [Accessed 7 June 2013].

Okin, S. (1999) Is Multiculturalism Bad For Women? *In*: Cohen, J., Howard, M. and Nussbaum, C. (eds) (1999) *Is Multiculturalism Bad For Women?* (New Jersey: Princeton University Press).

Oldham, J. (2014) Trojan Horse Jihadist Plot to Take Over Birmingham Schools. *Birmingham Mail*. 7 May, Available at: http://www.birminghammail.co.uk/news/midlands-news/trojan-horse-jihadist-plot-take-6782881 [Accessed May 2014].

Osler, A. (2007) *Faith Schools and Community Cohesion* (London: Runnymede Trust).

Osler, A. and Starkey, H. (2000) Citizenship, Human Rights and Cultural Diversity. *In*: Osler, A. (ed.) (2000) *Citizenship Democracy in Schools: Diversity, Identity and Equality* (Stoke on Trent: Trentham Books).

Osler, A. and Starkey, H. (2005) *Changing Citizenship: Democracy and Inclusion in Education* (Milton Keynes: Open University Press).

Ouseley, H. (2001) *Community Pride, Not Prejudice – Making Diversity Work in Bradford* (Bradford: Bradford Vision).

Parekh, B. (2000) *Rethinking Multiculturalism: Cultural Diversity and Political Theory* (Basingstoke: Macmillan).

Park, R.E. and Burgess, E.W. (1969) *Introduction to the Science of Sociology* (Chicago: University of Chicago Press).

Parker-Jenkins, M., Haratas, D. and Irving, B.A. (2005) *In Good Faith: Schools, Religion and Public Funding* (Aldershot: Ashgate).

Pauley, R. (2004) *Islam in Europe: Integration or Marginalization?* (Aldershot: Ashgate).

Peach, C. (2006) Islam ethnicity and South Asian Religions in the London 2001 Census. *Transaction*. 31 (3) 353–370.

Peach, C., Robinson, V. and Smith, S. (1981) *Ethnic Segregation in Cities* (London: Croom Helm).

Phillips, A. (2007) *Multiculturalism without Culture* (Princeton: Princeton University Press).

Philips, T. (2005) After 7/7: Sleep Walking to Segregation, Speech to the Manchester Council for Community Relations, 22 September. Available at: www.equalityhumanrights.com [Accessed January 2009].

Philips, R. (ed.) (2010) *Muslim Spaces of Hope: Geographies of Possibilities in Britain and the West* (London: Zed Books).

Philips, D. Simpson, L. and Ahmed, S. (2008) Shifting Geographies of Minority Ethnic Settlement: Remaking Communities in Oldham and Rochdale. *In*: Flint, J. and Robinson, D. (eds) *Community Cohesion in Crisis? New Dimensions of Diversity and Difference* (Bristol: Policy Press).

Philips, R. and Iqbal, J. (2010) Muslims and the Anti-war Movements. *In*: Philips, R (ed.) (2010) *Muslim Spaces of Hope: Geographies of Possibilities in Britain and the West* (London: Zed Books).

Platt, L. (2005) *Migration and Social Mobility* (York: Joseph Rowntree Foundation).

Poole, E. (2002) *Reporting Islam: Media Representations of British Muslims* (London: I.B.Tauris).

Potter, J. and Wetherall, M. (2010) *Discourse & Social Psychology* (London: Sage).

Poynting, S. and Mason, V. The Resistible Rise of Islamophobia: Anti-Muslim Racism in the UK and Australia before 9/11. *Journal of Sociology.* 43 (1) 61–86.

Pring, R. (2008) The Common School and the Comprehensive Ideal: A Defence. *In*: Halstead, J.M. and Haydon, G. (eds) (2008) *The Common School and the Comprehensive Ideal* (London: Wiley Blackwell).

Pring, R. (2009) Can Faith Schools Serve the Common Good? *In*: Haydon, G. (ed.) (2009) *Faith in Education: A Tribute to Terence McLaughlin* (London: Institute of Education).

Putnam, R. (2000) *Bowling Alone – The Collapse and Revival of American Community* (London: Touchstone).

Rabi, M. (1967) *The Political Theory of Ibn Khaldun* (Leiden: Brill).

Ramadan, T. (2004) *Western Muslims and the Future of Islam* (Oxford: Oxford University Press).

Ramadan, T. (2009) *Radical Reform: Islamic Ethics and Liberation* (Oxford: Oxford University Press).

Rambaut, R. (1997) Assimilation and its Discontents. *International Migration Review.* 31 (4) 923–960.

Reddie, R.S. (2009) *Black Muslims in Britain: Why Are a Growing Number of Young Black People converting to Islam?* (London: Lion).

Rawls, J. (1999) *A Theory of Justice* (Cambridge: MA: Harvard University Press).

Report Magazine (2009) Association of Teachers and Lecturers Magazine, June/July 2009 (London).

Ritchie, D. (2001) *Oldham Independent Review: One Oldham, One Future* (Manchester: Government Office for the North West).

Robinson, D. (2005) The Search for Community Cohesion: Key Themes and Dominant Concepts of the Public Policy Agenda. *Urban Studies.* 42 (8) 1411–1427.

Rosser, Ian (2005) Pupils in Class War II, *Yorkshire Evening Post,* 18 October.

Roy, O. (2004) *Globalised Islam: The Search for a New Ummah* (London: Hurst and Company).

Runnymede Trust (1997) *Islamophobia: A Challenge for Us All* (London: Runnymede Trust).

Runnymede Trust (2004) *Islamophobia: Issues, Challenges and Action* (London: Trentham Books).

Ryan, C. (2008) History of School Academies in Academies and the Future of State Schools. *In*: Astle, J and Ryan, C. (eds) *Academies and the Future of State Schools* (London: Centre Forum).

Safi, O. (ed.) (2003) *Progressive Muslims: On Gender Justice and Pluralism* (London: One World).

Said, E. (1978) *Orientalism* (London: Routledge).

Said, E. (1994) *Representation of the Intellectual* (London: Vintage).

Said, E. (1999) *Out of Place: A Memoir* (London: Granta).

Said, E. (2001) *Reflections on Exile* (London: Penguin).Santios, A. (2004) Embodying Ambivalence: Muslim Australians as 'Other'. *Journal of Australian Studies.* 82 49–153.

Sardar, Z. (1998) *Postmodernism and the Other: The New Imperialism of Western Culture* (London: Pluto Press).

Sardar, Z. (1999) *Orientalism* (Milton Keynes: Open University Press).

Sardar, Z. (2009) Spaces of Hope: Interventions. *In*: Philips, R. (ed.) (2010) *Muslim Spaces of Hope: Geographies of Possibilities in Britain and the West* (London: Zed Books).

Savage, M., Devine, F., Cunningham, N., Taylor, M., Li, Y., Le Roux, H.B., Friedman, S. and Miles, A. (2013) A New Model of Social Class: Findings from the BBC's Great British Class Survey Experiment. *Sociology.* 47 (2) 219–251.

Seddon, M. (2010) Constructing Identities of 'Difference' and 'Resistance': The Politics of Being Muslim and British. *Social Semiotics.* 20 (5) 557–571.

Sewell, T. (1997) *Black Masculinities and Schooling: How do Black Boys Survive Schooling* (Stoke on Trent: Trentham Books).

Shain, F. (2003) *The Schooling and Identity of Asian Girls* (Stoke on Trent: Trentham Books).

Short, G. (2002) Faith-Based Schools: A threat to Social Cohesion? *Journal of Philosophy of Education.* 36 (4) 559–572.

Sikand, Y. (2002) *The Origins and Development of the Tablighi jam'aat: (1920–2000). A Cross-country Comparative Study* (New Delhi: Orient Longman).

Simpson, L. (2004) Statistics of Racial Segregation: Measures, Evidence and Policy. *Urban Studies.* 41 (3) 661–681.

Simpson, L. (2012) *More Segregation or More Mixing?* Joseph Rowntree Founda-tion & University of Manchester. ESRC Centre on Dynamics of Ethnicity (Code).

Smithers R. (2005) Anger at Muslim Schools Attack Claims by Education Chief 'derogatory'. *The Guardian*, 18 January. Available at: http://www.guardian.co.uk/uk/2005/jan/18/schools.faithschools [Accessed 12 September 2010].

Stables, A. (2003) Schools as Imagined Community in Discursive Space: A Per-spective on the School Effectiveness Debate. *British Educational Research Journal*. 29 (6) 895–902.

Stephen, W. and Fegan, J.R. (eds) (1980) *School Desegregation: Past Present and Future* (New York: Plenum Publishing).

Straw, J. (2006) I Felt Uneasy Talking to Someone I Couldn't See, *The Guardian*; 6 October.

Swann Report (1985) *Education for All* (London: Her Majesty's Stationery Office).

Taylor, C. (1992) Multiculturalism and the Politics of Recognition. *In*: Guttman, A. (ed.) (1992) *Multiculturalism and the Politics of Recognition* (Princeton: Princeton University Press).

Taylor, C. (2009) *A Good School For Every Child: How to Improve Our Schools* (London: Routledge).

Taylor, G.D. (1986) *Public Opinion and Collective Action: The Boston de-Segregation Conflict* (Chicago: Chicago University Press).

Thomas, P. (2003) Young People, Community Cohesion and the Role of Youth Work in Building Social Capital. *Youth and Policy*. (81) 21–43.

Thomas, P. (2009) Between Two Stools? The Government's 'Preventing Violent Extremism' Agenda. *The Political Quarterly*. 80 (2) 282–291.

Thomas, P. (2011) *Youth, Multiculturalism and Community Cohesion* (Basingstoke: Palgrave).

Tomlinson, S. (2008) *Race and Education Policy* (New York: Open University Press).

Tough, P. (2008) *Whatever it Takes: Geoffrey Canada's Quest to Change Harlem and America* (New York: Houghton Mifflin Harcourt).

Troyna, B. (2003) *Bussing*, In Ellis Cashmore (Ed) *Encyclopedia of Race and Ethnic Studies* (London: Routledge).

Van-Dijk, T.A. (1993) *Elite Discourse and Racism* (London: Sage Publications).

Vasagar, J. (2013) *Michael Gove to send copy of King James Bible to all English schools*. Available at: http://www.theguardian.com/politics/2011/nov/25/michael-gove-king-james-bible [Accessed on January 2015].

Vertovec, S. (2007) Super-diversity and Its Implications. *Ethnic and Racial Studies*. 29 (6) 1024–1054.

Wagner, U. Christ, O. Pettigrew, T. Stellermacher, J. and Wolf, C. (2006) Prejudice and Monority Propotion. *Social Psychology Quarterly*. 69 (4), 380–390.

Weekes-Bernard, D. (2007) *School Choice and Ethnic Segregation: Education Decision-making among Black and Minority Parents* (London: Runnymede Trust).

Weeks, T. (2006) *From Assimilation to Anti-Semitism. The Jewish Question in Poland 1850–1914* (Northern Illinois: University Press).

Wells, A.S., Holme, J.J., Rivilla, A.T. and Atanda, AK. (2005) *'How De-segregation Changes Us': The Effects of Racially Segregated School*. Available at: http://cms. tc.columbia.edu/i/a/782_ASWells041504.pdf [Accessed February 2010].

Wernber, P. (2001) Divided Loyalties, Empowered Citizenship? Muslims in Britain. *Citizenship Studies*. 4 (3) 307–324.

West, A. (1994) Choosing Schools – The Consumers Perspective. *In*: Halstead, J.M. (ed.) (1994) *Parental Choice and Education: Principles, Policy and Practice* (London: Kogan Page).

West, A., Hind, A. and Pennell, H. (2004) School Admissions and 'Selection' in Comprehensive Schools: Policy and Practice. *Oxford Review of Education*. 30 (3) 347–369.

Wilshaw, M. (2014) 'Trojan horse' schools: Sir Michael Wilshaw's letter to Michael Gove. Available at: http://www.theguardian.com/education/2014/jun/09/trojan-horse-schools-wilshaw-ofsted-gove. [Accessed on 9 June, 2014].

Woods, P.A., Woods, G.J. and Gunter, H. (2007) Academy Schools and Entrepreneurialism in Education. *Journal of Education Policy*. 22 (2) 237–259.

Worley, C. (2005) 'It's not about Race. It's All about the Community': New Labour and Community Cohesion. *Critical Social Policy*. 25 (4) 483–496.

Young, R. (2003) *Post Colonialism: A Very Short Introduction* (New York: Oxford University Press).

Index

.

Printed and bound by CPI Group (UK) Ltd, Croydon, CR0 4YY